BELIEVE

Published by Grammar Factory Publishing, an imprint of MacMillan Company
Limited.

Grammar Factory Publishing
MacMillan Company Limited
25 Telegram Mews, 39th Floor, Suite 3906
Toronto, Ontario, Canada
M5V 3Z1

www.grammarfactory.com

James, Brenda
Believe: How New Leaders Step Up and Into Their Full Potential / Brenda James.

Paperback ISBN 978-1-98973-772-9
Hardcover ISBN 978-1-98973-774-3
eBook ISBN 978-1-98973-773-6
Audiobook ISBN 978-1-98973-775-0

   1. SEL044000 SELF-HELP / Self-Management / General. 2. BUS071000 BUSI-
NESS & ECONOMICS / Leadership. 3. BUS107000 BUSINESS & ECONOMICS /
Personal Success.

Production Credits
Cover design by Designerbility
Interior layout design by Dania Zafar
Book production and editorial services by Grammar Factory Publishing

Grammar Factory's Carbon Neutral Publishing Commitment
Grammar Factory Publishing is proud to be neutralizing the carbon footprint of
all printed copies of its authors' books printed by or ordered directly through
Grammar Factory or its affiliated companies through the purchase of Gold Stan-
dard-Certified International Offsets.

Disclaimer
The material in this publication is of the nature of general comment only and
does not represent professional advice. It is not intended to provide specific
guidance for particular circumstances, and it should not be relied on as the basis
for any decision to take action or not take action on any matter which it covers.
Readers should obtain professional advice where appropriate, before making
any such decision. To the maximum extent permitted by law, the author and
publisher disclaim all responsibility and liability to any person, arising directly or
indirectly from any person taking or not taking action based on the information
in this publication.

BELIEVE

HOW NEW LEADERS STEP UP AND INTO THEIR FULL POTENTIAL

BRENDA JAMES

TESTIMONIALS

BELIEVE is not a book you read once. It's a life-long friend you return to in moments that matter. A sacred space to find solace, inspiration and a pathway back to your brilliant self.

As the world grows more complex and our work demands more of our unique perspective, it's essential we know who we *really* are and what we're *really* capable of. This book is the antidote to any unconscious, disempowering thoughts and beliefs we might have that are holding us back from doing our best work and living our best life.

Brenda has an astonishing ability to make the esoteric realm of self-enquiry and self-awareness more accessible. She has a gift for illuminating simple, practical pathways that lead us to powerful personal insight. I cannot think of a more important conversation we need to be having right now.

If we're to be effective as leaders, we need to know who we are in order to grow who we are. This book will show you how. Hot tip – get extra copies for your friends and colleagues.

**Mykel Dixon, Award-winning Author and Speaker |
Creativity, Culture, Leadership**

Brenda's reflections and practical tools take you on a wonderful personal journey to first understand, then believe in, and finally embrace your authentic self, unlocking your true potential as a leader.

Fiona Kingsford, CEO, Board Director

Brenda captures wonderfully the tension between discovering how you are wired and, at the same time, trying to grow into the person you want to be. The book is full of great stories that demonstrate the challenges that we can all face trying to become leaders, with exercises to get you thinking differently about how to do this successfully. BELIEVE is an engaging road map to becoming the human-centric leader that you have always wanted to be.

Rajan Hira, Associate and Registered Architect | Chow:Hill Architects

BELIEVE helped me learn so much about myself in areas where a few tweaks can have such a huge impact. I could not see where to make these changes myself as I was so deep in the work, but this book has encouraged me to delve beneath the surface. I am back in control of my time and so much more self-aware, which has done great things for my emotional intelligence. I now trust my own judgement, which has excelled my learning, and most importantly, I can be myself – an honest and authentic leader. Amazing!

Darrin Madgwick, General Manager | UBP Direct

Aren't we all trying to figure life out, one decision at a time? While the decision to believe in yourself seems like a no-brainer, the stats show we're rubbish at it. This book will get you thinking and reflecting on what version of yourself you're being and how effective that really is.

Through a mix of real-life workplace scenarios, practical frameworks, and thought-provoking questions, you'll be guided towards harnessing the power of your potential.

Follow the workbook and you'll soon be stepping into the leader you were always meant to be. A book for every leader wanting to be better, and for every leader wanting to foster a legacy of leadership.

Rebecca Clarke FRCSA, Manager – New Zealand & Digital Community | RCSA

BELIEVE deserves to be fully embraced by every person responsible for performance, in any walk of life. If leaders and team members apply the learnings here with rigour and enthusiasm, most if not all will see an exceptional increase in productivity.

Sunil Prasad, Project Director | Universal Homes

CONTENTS

ABOUT THE AUTHOR

Brenda James is a leadership and career development specialist and the founder of Leadership Reboot. She coaches clients to three key outcomes: increased leadership confidence, more cohesive teams and higher workplace wellbeing.

Brenda is passionate about the freedom generated from believing in yourself because, like many, she wasn't always the thriving, self-assured businesswoman you see today. For decades Brenda was stuck in self-doubt and made destructive choices from a vulnerable place. Thankfully, with a lot of introspection and study, Brenda overcame her struggles and this is the inner strength she coaches from today.

She now has twenty years' coaching, recruitment and HR experience, a post-graduate qualification in career development, international accreditation in energy management and emotional intelligence, and a devoted passion for workplace and mental wellbeing.

But it's Brenda's inner strength that drives results. Believing in freedom for all, her mission is simple: to help leaders realise their professional purpose and potential. To take them back to self, values – belief!

She wholeheartedly believes there is a great leader already within each of you.

This book will show you exactly that.

Visit Brenda's website to access the **Believe Companion Workbook** at: www.leadership-reboot.co.nz/believe-companion-workbook

INTRODUCTION

As Emma walks up the stairs to her office, she feels a weird sensation in her belly. Her hands are a tad sweaty and her heart is beating faster than usual. She puts this down to the natural anxiety that comes with the first day in any new job. But she can't figure out why she feels so nervous. She's been at the top of her game for years now, so much so that her intuition guides her to do what she needs to get consistently high results. She's well respected within the company, so this feeling she has is brand new. Not something she remembers feeling before. Could it be self-doubt?

Later that morning, when Emma is introduced to her team as their new leader, a mix of expressionless faces and awkward smiles greets her. Just last week she was their colleague; now she's their boss. It feels as though their eyes are staring straight through her and that her nervousness is glaringly obvious. She can feel her face burning. The responsibility of being the leader is sinking in along with a whole lot of uncertainty about what lies ahead. For the first time she can remember, Emma feels small and inexperienced. Like the new kid on the block.

Being successful in her profession and progressing to leadership was the next organic career development step for Emma and a chance to help her team develop their careers by passing on what she's learned. But it's all brand new, and more than she anticipated. She didn't realise how much she's become used to hearing compliments for her excellent work and results. The cheerleaders have gone quiet. Sure, there is encouragement, but not the recognition she's used to.

As days and weeks pass, Emma's super-organised desk starts to look like a storm has just blown through the office. The number of interruptions increases: questions are asked by email, phone and any other way the team can track her down. By the end of her first month, the interruptions are louder and her workload heavier, with hardly any gaps in her calendar to do actual work.

Issues show up before the end of her second month. Seemingly out of the blue, the team bully rears her ugly head and creates conflict left, right and centre. That causes her most confident team member mental distress, prompting a complaint to Human Resources about Emma's leadership. That hardly feels fair. Those two had their issues way before Emma took over.

Then there is the repetitive issue of dwindling team performance on the last day of the week, with more focus on Friday night drinkies than a last push to reach weekly goals. Oh, and to top it all off, the one who competed with Emma for the leadership job has just offered her umpteenth opinion about what Emma should be doing to sort out her team. In all her observations of leaders and leadership styles, Emma has never seen this kind of mayhem.

If you are like Emma, then you have experienced both strong and poor leadership. You've known leaders who've done it well and those who haven't. You've felt it. You've found yourself critiquing others' leadership styles, particularly the poor role models.

You thought you had it figured out enough to at least get started.

You discover the hard way that observing from a distance and actually doing leadership are streets apart. You notice a niggling voice getting louder in your head. When you leave meetings, you question yourself. 'Why did I say that?' 'Why did I say it **like** that?' 'Ugh, that was so not leadership-like.'

Self-doubt grows and belief fades. You feel hypersensitive and certain that others will soon see that you just don't have what it takes to be a good leader. Who can you trust with the intricate details of such private thoughts? You don't know who to talk to. Certainly not your peers, who make leadership look effortless.

With ridiculous deadlines to meet and struggling to stay on top, you hold tight to your workload, working harder and longer. Your to-do list is growing by the hour and the pressure is on from senior management for your team to perform. There is no let up. A few months back, all you had to do was get your own work done, tick one thing after another off your to-do list and watch the results roll in.

Whatever the flavour of your own issues is, the one certainty is that you're starting to feel like you are stuck in a pressure cooker that is about to blow.

Your increasing self-doubt moves into overwhelm and you start wondering if you are even on the right career path, repeatedly waking at 2am trying to figure out how to sort it all out. Questioning your every move, you have a constant feeling in your gut that you need to stop and reassess how you are working, but there is no time to pause.

New leaders go from getting frequent feedback and appreciation to feeling like a very small fish in a big, brand-new pond.

YOU ARE NOT ALONE

When things are new or getting tough, we start doubting ourselves. Stressing, worrying, imagining how things can go wrong. What I'm about to tell you may feel bittersweet, but it's not just you who has felt this way.

Eighty-five per cent of new and developing leaders suffer similar scenarios. In fact, many veteran leaders do too.

- Why does leadership create so much pressure?
- When did humans become so complex?
- Where did all these problems appear from and what the hell are you meant to do?
- Which course, which book, which coach: Who can you trust to ask for help?

It's time to stop asking yourself:

- Am I good enough?
- Why did I say that?
- Why can't I just fix this?
- What is the point if I can't even do this one little thing?
- I wonder if they know I have no idea what I'm doing?

All those questions will do is take you further down the rabbit hole and it will be harder to climb back out.

No matter where or when you started to experience a dent in your self-belief, once it is triggered and activated, your outlook changes. You see everything through blurred lenses. You constantly look for evidence that you are not quick enough, deserving enough or smart enough. And, of course, you always find it.

Not believing in yourself will totally affect your ability to reach your full potential.

BEEN THERE, DONE THAT!

It was my own story that inspired me to write this book to help others take control of the script and write their own career story.

I've been there with those constant feelings of not being quick enough, deserving enough or smart enough. I wasn't always the thriving, self-assured businesswoman people see today. For decades, I was plagued by feelings of self-doubt – letting destructive choices rule my life.

The great news is – what was once a source of pain for me is now my superpower. I confronted my own struggles head on after a poignant meeting that became one of several turning points for me.

I was in a meeting with the CEO of the company I was working for, having one of our regular catch-ups. On this day, she gave me a piece of feedback that I have never forgotten. She said I was behaving with bravado. 'What's bravado?' I asked her, eyebrows raised. I genuinely did not know what the word meant.

Despite being a high performer in my profession, my self-belief was weak. I had a long list of things that triggered my self-doubt, which were buried deep but ignited easily. I saw my failures a lot quicker than any success.

I continually searched for answers. I read dozens of books, attended courses, and even walked on fire as part of a personal development weekend. I invested a lot of money searching for belief and it was worth it, if temporary results were all I was after. Every single time, after a brief reprieve, my self-doubt would return with vengeance.

No matter how many times the CEO said I was smart, amazing at my job, that I had a lot to offer, and that people looked up to me, it wouldn't register on my self-belief scale. I could not bring myself to believe her. So, I overcompensated. You know that saying 'Fake it till you make it?' That is exactly what I did, with concentrated effort.

Turns out, I did not present as self-assured at all in that meeting. More like cocky, overconfident and sometimes arrogant – the classic description of *bravado*. I was quietly devastated as I heard her words. I felt embarrassment working its way up my body. It started as a sick feeling in my tummy, moved to a more intense tightness in my chest, then, finally, a burning redness in my face. I was sure I was going to cry.

As I grappled with the emotion I was feeling and tried hard not to show her how upset I was, I soon noticed a gentle but persistent shift within my mind and emotions. A feeling of quiet determination to learn how to change this.

I didn't know it then, but this was a turning point for me. I learned first-hand the value of **choice**. I embarked on a decade-long journey of internally targeted self-development that brought me to where I am now. My self-belief is deep and lasting. It's from this place of belief that I can help leaders just like you navigate your own path towards happy, assured leadership.

Ask yourself these questions honestly.
1. Have you ever felt alone or isolated about leadership pressure?
2. Are you experiencing anxiety or self-doubt?
3. Do you doubt you will instinctively say and do the right things as a leader?
4. Are you ready to change?

If you answered yes to two or more of those questions, great! Why? Because not believing in yourself as a leader can have a dramatic effect on more than just leadership. It can infiltrate your career and your life outside of work. It will impact those closest to you and negatively influence your relationships, even those you are leading.

It is time to make your own crucial 'choice'.
- Do you want to stay where you are? Or…
- Do you want to progress and step into your full potential, as a leader and as a human?

The fact you are still reading shows that you are curious. You want to progress. You want to grow. To grow personally and professionally, you need to be willing to take a few calculated risks and push through roadblocks.

It is time to step outside of your comfort zone and beyond what you thought you were capable of. But safely, with guidance, step by step.

HOW TO USE THIS BOOK

This book will take you on a private journey. Treat it as your own personal guide that will safely lead you to all the answers you have been looking for. Embrace the process and let its wisdom equip you with one of the key fundamentals of leadership – self-belief.

Chapter by chapter, you'll be taken through a method of introspection. Looking within. There are simple action steps along the way and tools to help you shine a light on all the reasons why you should believe in yourself as a leader.

They may seem wildly different or perhaps just slightly different to what you've done in your life and leadership career up until this point. That will depend on you.

So let's begin.

WHY BELIEVE?

It is the second time Doug has given the same instruction to Mike and the second time Mike has returned with the wrong result. Doug is tearing his hair out. Why isn't Mike listening?!

The team is incredibly busy working towards an intense deadline and Mike is holding things up. So, the third time Doug is instructing Mike, he decides to sit down in a private meeting room and show Mike step by step how he himself learned this task years ago. He prints off examples, he slows down his speech and he takes Mike through the task instructions again. Mike shows refreshing enthusiasm and understanding this time, which is a promising sign. Doug is hopeful.

Fast-forward two days when Mike brings the completed task back to Doug. This time, Doug can't hide his exasperation. It is wrong. In fact, it's worse than the last two attempts. With the deadline looming, Doug has no option but to work overtime and just get it done.

Despite his earlier hope, deep down, Doug isn't surprised his instructions haven't worked. He feels like he is failing miserably at this leadership thing. He should have just done it himself in the first place. All this experience has done is make him doubt himself even more.

When it comes to figuring out how to be a better leader, Doug does a lot of searching, thinking that finding the *right technique or tactic* holds the key to his leadership success. He can't understand why the things he's discovered aren't working. He finds a new *tactic* and thinks 'this is it', but inevitably the new 'this' becomes the latest thing that doesn't work. Despite Doug's searching, he never does land on the right answer. In fact, all his searching and seeking deceives him, misleading him down a rabbit hole.

As a high performer, Doug excelled in his role for many years and it felt as though anything he touched turned to gold. If he didn't know how to do something, he searched until he found out how and got on with it. He can't understand why that has worked for him but not for his team. The problem is that Doug doesn't believe in himself as a leader; he can try all the tactics he wants, but the results will ultimately be the same.

If only he knew that he is already a great leader. This is why he was promoted in the first place. If only he knew that without self-belief, the external stuff he is discovering and trying repeatedly will not return lasting results.

When you continually search for answers outside yourself, which you possibly already do, you are likely to find many paths that lead you to discovering how to be a better leader. How to develop a productive team, be an effective problem solver, become more decisive, be a better communicator and influencer. You can find the best time management system in the world to cope with doing your own job alongside leading a team. Some solutions may even work, if only for a while.

In fact, if you Google 'learning about leadership' you will get over seventy-one million results – anything from academic leadership theories to twenty things you should do and ten things you shouldn't do as a new leader. The list of topics and potential solutions can go on infinitely. You become fixated on finding answers, so much so that you get further and further away from where the most profound answers lie.

As humans we tend to make things more complicated than they need to be. Searching for answers to 'fix' us. I'm sure you have tried your share of solutions so you can be a better leader, communicator, problem solver or delegator. When you find one solution, you don't stop there. You try it again and again, expecting the result to be different. When it isn't, you keep searching, adding layer after layer. You are left wondering why all this stuff isn't working for you. Just as Doug keeps wondering why Mike isn't listening to his instructions.

If you are waiting to hear how Doug sorts things out with Mike, great. Here it is... Doug eventually discovers that he's been looking in the wrong direction. That he needs to turn his searchlight around and point it inwards. Yes, external solutions can be great, but only after you have developed inner strength and self-belief. Believing in yourself means having a strong sense of self and confidence in your own abilities. It's about you. The answers aren't out there somewhere. Believing in yourself comes from within you. Then you will find your leadership strength.

———————————

It's time to change tack completely. To stop looking out there and start looking within.

———————————

FACE FACTS

Have you ever been to the doctor with a persistent pain or issue and been given a pill? The pill fixes the pain, but within a week of finishing the course of pills, the pain returns. Only this time it's worse. After another visit to the doctor, you are prescribed more pills. This time you add the side effects of heartburn and being tired all the time to your list of symptoms. What do you do now? Go back to the doctor and ask for more pills?

What happened here is that your doctor didn't find or treat the actual cause of your complaint. They simply put a plaster over the real issue. Masked it – but only for a while.

It's exciting to think there is a magical answer out there to help you instantly connect with your belief and all you need to do is stumble upon it. The problem is, when you look outside of yourself for answers, you are doing exactly what the doctor did. Putting a plaster over the real issue. Such temporary fixes help you momentarily escape the pain or the plaguing anxiety or self-doubt, but you are depriving yourself of an opportunity to experience long-lasting success.

Masking the symptoms will not work in the long term. In leadership, things are going to come at you from many angles and it is highly likely you will be triggered at some point in your leadership journey. Emotionally triggered, that is. If you have any self-doubt sitting just beneath the surface, then as a leader, it will be activated and race to the surface in a heartbeat. When you lack belief, you look for evidence that your self-doubt is right, so you find it.

Being able to **believe** in yourself is an undervalued trait that influences every part of life. In fact, research shows that self-belief helps in the release of serotonin, a hormone that helps your mind and body to relax and think clearly. Pity the doctor can't prescribe that, because thinking clearly helps stimulate reasoning and problem-solving skills that help in thinking outside the box and being more creative. All great for leadership success. All offshoots of belief.

First, you need to take a pause from looking outside of yourself for answers. In fact, pause and do that right now. Take the deepest breath you can, hold it for three to four seconds, then sigh out the loudest sigh you can manage. Don't worry about who can see or hear you. Do it again. Now one more time. Even deeper and louder. Relaxing, right? Consider these your first sighs of relief because you are in the right place.

A great leader is already within you.

When you are driven to perform from deep within yourself, you will do your best work, meet your full potential and feel good about it. You'll stop asking yourself all those questions like 'Am I good enough?' and 'Why did I say that?' and replace them with 'I've got this,' 'I did the best I could in that moment,' and 'I'm becoming a better leader every day.' You'll be triggered less. Sleep through the night! You'll let go of more, yet feel more in control.

Then there are the trickle-down effects on your circle of influence. When your team feel your belief, they will believe in you too. They'll more willingly invest their time, energy and loyalty so that both you and they are successful. You'll lead them with assurance and direction. You'll teach them the value of believing in themselves by 'being' an inspiring role model.

It's time to move from a place of insignificance and struggle. Now is your time to thrive and fulfil your potential. To make an impact.

To understand how to do this, let's first look at someone who encapsulates it well.

FROM INSIGNIFICANCE TO INFLUENCE

Oprah Winfrey is a great example of someone with inner strength and truth. She is much more than a television talk show host.

She is one of the world's most powerful business leaders, who exerts a great deal of influence on mainstream society.

She has a magnetic energy that pulls you in and keeps you captivated. She owns her presence, the space around her. It's not the words she speaks, but the force that carries them that makes us sit up and listen.

Oprah has come a long way from rural Mississippi, where she was born. To say that she is a black woman from the South who overcame the odds would be a huge understatement. Her battles didn't begin with her race or gender, but rather with a turbulent adolescence in the small farming community of Kosciusko.

After moving to Nashville to live with her father, Oprah started at Tennessee State University in 1971 before moving to Baltimore, then Maryland five years later to begin her career in television. By 1986, Oprah had her own nationally syndicated television program – *The Oprah Winfrey Show*. This was the platform that catapulted her to critical acclaim and global recognition. There was a time when none of us knew her. Now she wows the world.

According to Forbes, Oprah was the richest African American of the 20th century. *Life* magazine also recognised her as the most influential woman of her generation, a testament to this media icon who has not only done it all but inspired an entire generation of young women to pursue their dreams – regardless of their race or ethnicity.

Oprah can inspire an audience with the way she articulates her point of view on success with unparalleled authority: 'I sit here profitable, successful, by all definitions of the word. But what really, really resonates deeply with me is that I live a fantastic life; my inner life is really intact. I live from the inside out. Everything I have, I have because I let it be fuelled by who I am and what I realise my contributions to the planet could be.'

Oprah credits her success to her commitment in creating that indestructible inner strength. And you can feel it. When Oprah speaks, her conviction and belief system shine through. Her strength comes from having an inner sanctuary that is immune to the external world. She doesn't get lost in her success and she is untouched by the inevitable tragedies and failures that are part of any life. She is grounded in that sanctuary of hers and it shows.

———————————

Having inner strength is like having an unshakeable core. That inner strength is your precondition for success.

———————————

Now, obviously not all of us can become Oprah! But when you genuinely believe in yourself, you will step up and into your full potential as a leader – whether that's in sales, administration, architecture and construction, science, health or an executive role. Whatever industry or specialisation, inner strength will serve you.

You don't have to be Oprah, but when you learn to believe in yourself your whole world opens up and you can make a positive impact, as Figure 2.1 shows.

Five Steps from Insignificance to **Influence**

IMPACT

Confidence

Self-awareness

Desire to change

Self-doubt

Figure 2.1: From insignificance to influence

FIGURE 2.1 EXPLAINED

As you move up one step to the next, you will find yourself gathering momentum, feeling stronger and energised. The view will be broader and clearer, just as it is with any ladder you climb.

Step One – Self-doubt: Self-doubt shows up when you lack confidence or feel incapable of doing the things you need to do. When you are doubting yourself, you feel insignificant. You experience uncertainty around things you can't control or worry about things not going according to plan. It can be a crippling place to be and it is almost impossible to influence from this frame of mind. If you can't move from here, it's unlikely you'll see any change. The best thing that could happen is that you are forced into a corner that ignites an inner yearning that launches you to step two.

Step Two – Desire to change: When you arrive at step two – celebrate! You are exactly where you need to be. The desire to change is an uncomfortable place to land and usually comes about because you can no longer live with the way things are. The stronger your desire to change is the better, because change takes honesty, open mindedness and willingness. You will need a conviction that the change you seek is necessary and that you truly want it. This will give you the energy and drive to reach step three.

Step Three – Self-awareness: This is where you will explore nooks and crannies that you've never had the courage to peek into before. Why? Because, if you do what you've always done, you'll get what you've always got. It's time to look in a different direction – within. Getting to know yourself is where the rubber hits the road, where the real work begins. From what you think to how you react, uncovering blind spots and understanding emotions, getting to know **you** will give you an inner strength you've never known and springboard you to step four.

Step Four – Confidence: Once you know yourself deeper, the next step is learning to trust what you now know because when you trust yourself, you develop a kinder and more confident inner voice. Before you know it, you are operating from an intuitive space and making sound judgements. Leading with this level of confidence and flow, you naturally become more trustworthy, which is one of the key ingredients to developing a trusting team. Win win!

Step Five – Impact: You've now put helpful tools in your toolkit to support you in not only stepping into your full leadership potential, but being able to stay there. Self-care is integrated as one of your priorities, as is letting your new and improved leadership self shine. This will lead you to instinctively influence more accountability and productivity and make a positive impact in your day-to-day leadership work.

Think about where you are right now. Which step? Then think about where you want to be. Because you might be at a place where you are doubting yourself right now, but working on your belief is a practice and a process that will energise you to take each 'next' step.

I encourage you to pause for five minutes. Sit quietly and take a moment to reframe your thinking. Move away from thinking about where you are now to where you want to be.

Why do you need to **believe** – in you? I've started the list off for you, but add to it to make it uniquely yours. It will inspire you to keep moving forward.

———————

Self-belief is the positive feeling you have inside telling you that you are capable of anything. And those who don't have it probably let many things go by undone.

———————

WHY I NEED TO BELIEVE	
DO YOU WANT TO STAY HERE?	OR DO YOU WANT TO BE HERE?
I feel weighed down by self-doubt.	I'm excited about the possibility of making a change.
I feel stuck.	I'm ready now and open to learning a new way.
I have no idea where to start.	Knowing myself gives me an inner strength I never knew before.
I don't know how to inspire my team.	I'm influencing others by being my authentic self.

Now that you have this list, know where you're at and know where you want to get to, it's time to dive in and learn how to **believe** in three easy parts:

- Know yourself deeper
- Learn to trust yourself
- Embrace and be your true self

That is what we are going to explore next.

PART 1:

KNOW YOURSELF

'He who knows others is wise. He who knows himself is enlightened.'
Lao Tzu

How well do you think you know yourself? **Really** know yourself. Deeply. Why do you think and behave the way you do? What drives you? What irks you? How well do you know your strengths, weaknesses, likes and dislikes? Your thought patterns and default feelings? What about your flaws, insecurities and doubts? What triggers you to laugh, frown or snap at another person in frustration?

Knowing yourself is about discovering who you are as a person and as a leader. It is worth every moment of the self-study and reflection that you need to do. Worth every moment of analysing life experiences that brought you to where you are right now. Understanding how you relate to others. How you respond to people, places and things and how you handle emotions like stress and fear.

When you dig deeper like this and know yourself better, you can choose to change what you don't like and wholeheartedly embrace what you do like.

You'll be surprised at the staggering statistic about how many of us think we are self-aware when we are not. How often do you pause to notice your feelings, your physical sensations, your reactions, your habits, your behaviours and your thoughts?

The reality is that most of our thoughts and actions are on auto-pilot. Sometimes that's a good thing, but not always. Have you ever driven home while still thinking about work, and realised when you arrived home that you couldn't remember any of the drive? Autopilot works brilliantly for starting your car or sneez-ing, but it's not so great when you're manoeuvring twists and bends. When you're on autopilot for so long, you forget you're on autopilot, so before you know it you've developed a whole lot of habits, routines and impulses, and no longer control them – they control you.

So how do you get that perfect balance of being on autopilot and switching into manual when you need to? It can feel daunting, partly because self-awareness seems like such an intangible or abstract concept. But here's the thing. It is a skill anyone can improve. All you need is the right guidance and a little practice.

I break self-awareness down into three parts. Just like a tripod needs three legs to stand strong, self-awareness needs all three parts to be effective.

1. **Internal** self-awareness
2. **External** self-awareness
3. **Emotional** self-awareness

Right now, you don't know that you don't know what you don't know. Let's change that.

We're going to look at each part of self-awareness in more detail.

INTERNAL SELF-AWARENESS

When the eagle was very small, he fell from the safety of his nest. A chicken farmer found the eagle, brought him to the farm and raised him in a chicken coop with all his other chickens. The eagle grew up doing what chickens do, living like a chicken and believing he was a chicken.

A naturalist came to the chicken farm one day to see if what he had heard about an eagle acting like a chicken was really true. He was surprised to see the eagle strutting around the chicken coop, pecking at the ground and acting very much like a chicken.

The farmer explained to the naturalist that this bird was no longer an eagle. He was now a chicken because he'd been trained to be a chicken and he believed he was a chicken. The naturalist knew there was more to this great bird than his actions showed. He was born an eagle and had the heart of an eagle, and nothing could change that.

The man lifted the eagle onto the fence surrounding the chicken coop and said, 'You are an eagle. Stretch your wings and fly.' The eagle moved slightly, only to look at the man, then glanced down at his home among the chickens in the chicken coop where he was comfortable. He jumped off the fence and continued doing what chickens do. The farmer was satisfied. 'I told you it was a chicken,' he said.

The naturalist returned the next day and tried again to convince the farmer that the eagle was born for something greater. He took the eagle to the top of the farmhouse and spoke to him: 'You are an eagle. You belong in the sky. Stretch your wings and fly.' The large bird looked at the man, then again down into the chicken coop. He jumped from the man's arm onto the roof of the farmhouse.

Knowing what eagles are really about, the naturalist asked the farmer to let him try one more time. 'I'll come back tomorrow and prove that this bird is an eagle,' he said. The farmer, convinced otherwise, said, 'It is a chicken, but okay, if you must.' The naturalist returned the next morning to the chicken farm and took the eagle and the farmer some distance away to the foot of a high mountain. From here, they couldn't see the farm or the chicken coop.

The man held the eagle on his arm and pointed high into the sky where the bright sun was beckoning above. He spoke: 'You are an eagle! You belong in the sky. Stretch your wings and fly.' This time the eagle stared skyward into the bright sun, straightened his large body and stretched his massive wings. His wings moved, slowly at first, then surely and powerfully. With the mighty screech of an eagle, he flew.

Eagles are fearless and tenacious. They have incredible vitality and strength and are known for nurturing their young ones. Yet the small eagle lived for years thinking he was a chicken. He didn't soar the skies as eagles do. He didn't use his razor-sharp vision. He simply strutted around in a cage and timidly pecked at the ground.

—————————

The many leaders who suffer from a lack of self-belief fall into the trap of thinking that is just the way they are destined to be. But they are not.

—————————

LOOKING INWARD

We can all experience a decline in self-belief at work from time to time. Maybe, you come up with great ideas but struggle to make your voice heard in meetings. Or leadership isn't quite what you expected. To address dips in belief, you first need to go right back to the beginning and figure out what is causing the dips in the first place.

Getting to know yourself deeper – self-awareness – is often overlooked in business settings, yet it is the solid foundation from where to start your journey towards developing more belief in yourself. I'm not talking about strengths and weaknesses here. You can easily do a SWOT exercise. No doubt you have done one at some point in your career. What I'm talking about is having a deeper look within.

Getting to know yourself is where the rubber hits the road. It's where the real work begins. Remember I said you'll be surprised at the staggering statistic about how many of us think we are self-aware? That number is ninety-five per cent. Most of the population think they are self-aware, but in fact, only about fifteen per cent are. Repeat – only fifteen per cent!

Of course, we'd all like to believe we're self-aware and can probably find evidence that we are. But the facts point to a more sobering truth. Organisational psychologist Tasha Eurich has spent over four years researching what it truly means to be self-aware, and it's her research that returned the fifteen per cent statistic.

WHAT YOU THINK

Let's look at a basic example. Imagine you are lying in bed awake at 2am and you hear a loud bang. You instantly think it's a burglar, but you're too afraid to get up and look so you nervously lie awake most of the night. The next day you struggle with fatigue and everything feels like an upward climb. Interestingly, your neighbour hears the same loud bang at 2 am, but her first thought is that it's just the cat knocking something over. She goes straight back to sleep and wakes up refreshed and ready to face anything the day throws at her.

The event – the loud bang – was the same for both of you. What was different was what you thought about the loud bang. It's what we call perception, which is very powerful and influential in directing our thoughts and actions. In essence, it guides who we choose to be.

The National Science Foundation has been saying for decades that we have 50-70,000 thoughts per day and many scientists support this finding. But more recently, research by a team of psychology experts at Queen's University in Canada indicated we have 6,000 thoughts a day. Their team has developed a never-before-seen way to detect when one thought ends and another begins, and they wrote a paper outlining a method of isolating specific moments when a human is focused on a single idea. They described this phenomenon as a 'thought worm'.

Potentially both teams of researchers are right because science also shows that only one to five per cent of our thoughts are conscious thoughts, whereas the remaining ninety-five per cent are subconscious. Those are the thoughts that are tucked away beneath the surface, so we are not as aware of them, yet they are driving our every move.

Interestingly, it's often your subconscious thoughts that lead to things like fear, anxiety and self-doubt. It's highly likely that the 6,000 thought worms are your conscious thoughts: the one to five per cent. The ones you are more aware of. Leaving the remaining tens of thousands of thoughts being those you have while on autopilot: your subconscious thoughts.

The first step to increasing your self-awareness is increasing thought awareness. This is when you become aware of what's going on inside your mind. Our thoughts usually start the moment we open our eyes in the morning, and most of us are not aware of what our first thought is. Therefore, regardless of which scientist is right – those who say we have 6,000 thoughts per day or those who say we have 60,000 thoughts per day – we could all do with increasing our level of awareness about what we are thinking moment to moment. What I am suggesting, very strongly, is that you take action to become more aware of your thoughts, especially if you lack self-belief.

There is every chance that you have an overactive inner critic looming beneath the surface criticising who you are and what you do at every opportunity.

You can rather accurately assume that for at least part of the day, you are subconsciously telling yourself that you're a chicken, when in fact you are an eagle! Given that we have thousands of thoughts every day, imagine the damage you could be doing.

FORMING FILTERS

Thinking and thought is not a new topic. It has been talked about and written about for decades. An iconic book that comes to mind is *Think and Grow Rich* by Napoleon Hill, written way back in 1937. This book talks about success coming to those who think about success. Flip that around and failure comes to those who allow themselves to think mostly about failure. The object of Napoleon Hill's book was to help readers learn the art of changing their minds from failure to success consciousness. And guess where it starts? Thoughts and thinking.

Then there's Henry Ford and his famous quote: *'If you think you can or if you think you can't, you are right.'* Add to that Albert Einstein, who said, *'We cannot solve our problems with the same thinking we used to create them.'* I could go on and on and on. We really can bring about what we think about!

Here is a critical question.

What are you broadcasting to yourself, about yourself, through your thoughts from the moment you wake up in the morning? Do you even know?

If you are here reading this book, a book about developing more belief and stepping into your full potential, there's a high chance that your thoughts need to change. Especially the thoughts you have about **you**.

To prove to you how powerful thoughts are, just think back to the last time an old friend called or visited you out of the blue and your first comment was, 'Oh my goodness, I was just thinking about you!' What about when you decide it's time to buy a new car? You choose a blue Toyota and suddenly, during your regular outings, you see blue Toyotas everywhere. What's that about?

Our brains are incredibly complex machines that process millions of thoughts and data throughout every day – and night. To make sure that the system doesn't get overloaded and crash, it uses a filter. This filter is incredibly important because it determines the lens through which you view the world.

To a large degree, **you form this filter yourself** by telling your brain – *whether consciously or subconsciously* – what's important to you: what you believe and what you fear. Whether you think the loud bang at 2 am is a burglar or the neighbour's cat. Over time, through this process, you attract what you focus on. As John Lubbock said, *'What we see depends on what we look for.'*

So, if your thoughts are that powerful, that means that thoughts can hold you back. Especially thoughts that are flavoured with fear, self-doubt and worry. Worry takes thoughts to a whole new level. It's basically the thinking we do about all the things we don't want to happen or that we're afraid are going to happen. Some call worrying a dress rehearsal for failure.

It's not all bad, though. You will have days that are simply amazing, days where you feel motivated and happy, and if you explore your thoughts on those days, they are sure to be mostly positive.

JOURNALING YOUR THOUGHTS

The **thoughts journal** process I suggest has been tested on hundreds of leaders throughout a period of four years now, as part of our Leadership Essentials program. The consistent feedback from those who are committed to a week of thoughts reflection is: 'Wow, that was so insightful,' and 'I didn't realise how many negative thoughts I had.' Many are surprised at the thoughts they have about going into work each day. Some are pleasantly surprised by the positivity of their thought trends, but see some things that need to change.

I structured the journal to empower you to look at yourself objectively by performing daily self-reflection. Don't panic, I'm not asking you to keep a lengthy diary. A journal is different to a diary. Keeping a journal is focused on proactive personal evolution. The point of the exercise is to become more in tune with what you are thinking each day, then look back and reflect on it. It does not need to be a time-intensive task. Five minutes morning and night is all you need.

When you put your thoughts down on paper they become clearer and you are likely to see patterns that will explain some of your behaviours. I urge you not to underestimate the value of this exercise. Give it a go. Commit for seven days to observe your thoughts using this process.

Every morning, before you do anything else, write down your first thought for the day and then at least three things you are grateful for. If you forget to do this first thing, then start when you remember.

At the end of the day before going to sleep, reflect on your thinking patterns for the day, especially those thoughts about yourself as a leader. Then, for the last step, describe a situation or event that happened at work that day, what your thoughts were about that event, your perception, and how that led to your response.

Look for patterns in your thoughts that are driving your behaviour. Patterns you couldn't see before. There is a high chance that you notice negative thought patterns, especially in the way you think about **you**.

THOUGHTS REFLECTION

Use this reflection format each day for seven days. You can do it either in a notebook or in the **companion workbook**.

Morning insight
My first thought this morning was…
Today I am grateful for…
1.
2.
3.

Evening reflection
What I noticed about my thought patterns today was…

A significant event that happened today
To add another layer, think about an event that happened at work today that provoked a reaction from you.

What did you think about that event?
How did your thinking influence your response or reaction?

After seven days of journaling like this, it is highly likely you will begin to see patterns in your thoughts that are driving your behaviour. Perhaps patterns you couldn't see before. This is a great way to start rearranging your thoughts to be more constructive and helpful to you.

THE BRAIN'S ABILITY TO CHANGE

The great news is that once you are more aware of what you are thinking, you can change the pattern of your thoughts using one of your brain's natural, yet profound abilities called *neuroplasticity*.

For many years, scientists believed that the brain didn't change after childhood. That it was hardwired and fixed by the time we became adults. But advances in the last decade have shown that is not the case.

To understand how neuroplasticity works, think of your brain as a dynamic, connected power grid. There are billions of pathways, or roads, lighting up each time you think, feel or do something. Some of these roads are well travelled. These are your habits and habitual thoughts, your usual ways of thinking, feeling and doing. Every time you think in a certain way, practise a specific task or feel a particular emotion, you strengthen this road, which makes it easier for your brain to travel that pathway.

If you are a visual person, visualise a paddock of overgrown grass. You walk through the paddock once, lifting your foot high with each step and then putting it down, flattening the grass slightly. If you repeatedly walk the exact same path, the grass becomes flatter and flatter and becomes easier to walk on. Same thing with thinking. Every time you think, do or feel the same thing, the path is becoming easier to travel.

Say we want to think about something differently. Learn a new task or choose a different emotion. Such as change 'I can't do this,' to 'I will find a way to learn this.' We start carving out a new road in our brains. If we keep travelling that road, our brains begin to use this new pathway more and this new way of thinking, feeling or doing becomes second nature. The old pathway gets used less and less and weakens.

The **great news** is that we can all learn and change by rewiring our brains. If you have ever changed a bad habit or formed a new one by thinking about something differently, you have carved a new pathway in your brain and experienced neuroplasticity first-hand. With repeated and directed attention towards your desired change, you can rewire your brain.

As you continue to read this book, notice which are the more negative thoughts that come into your mind about your leadership journey. I encourage you to make a conscious effort to capture them, *using the thoughts journal process*, then make a conscious ***choice*** to change each of them to a more positive and empowering thought that will lead you to a more self-assured mindset. That is neuroplasticity in action.

Give yourself a chance to recognise negativity when it turns up, then have the strength to pause and make a better choice – before you react! Vicktor E. Frankl has a brilliant way of looking at the pause. He says that between stimulus and response there is a space; in that space lies your power to choose your response, and in your response lies your growth and your freedom. Powerful!

Pausing lessens the chances that you will react badly and be thrown by things that happen to and around you. You will have more capacity to connect with the power that lies in the space, to choose your response and to shrug things off. One of my favourite coaches called shrugging things off my *Teflon coating*. Thought awareness gave me the strength to remain a step ahead. The Teflon coating works much better that way.

———————————

At worst, internal self-awareness helps leaders rise to new levels of credibility and effectiveness for themselves. At best, the sky's the limit for you, your team and the entire organisation.

———————————

FORMING NEW PATHWAYS

Sue is an architect and project team leader who runs large, complex and long-term construction projects. Site meetings are a regular occurrence with the construction team. She always used to feel uncomfortable in the lead up to site meetings and, in her words, 'a real mess' after the meetings. They were a gruff and stubborn bunch, often questioning parts of her design and wanting to do things differently. She'd feel her voice shaking as she spoke and was sure everyone else was aware of it.

When Sue used the *thoughts journal* tool to reflect on her thoughts, specifically relating to these meetings, she had a profound insight that led to a major **aha** moment.

First, a little backstory about Sue. She is a considered thinker, and has a quiet personality and a high level of empathy, meaning she avoids conflict like the plague. She often felt unheard because to get herself heard she needed to speak up loudly. Louder than she was comfortable with.

The thoughts reflection made it obvious to Sue that by speaking up loudly, and often having to repeat herself more than once to be heard, she felt aggressive, which went against the grain of her natural compassion. It didn't feel right to Sue and she often left the meetings feeling very uncomfortable.

Becoming aware of her thought trends has changed the way Sue approaches the meetings. Before heading into a more complex site meeting, she now allows five minutes in her calendar to be still and recognise what thoughts are whirring around in her head. She is aware of what will push her emotional buttons and reminds herself that this project is important, her design is exceptional and if the shaking happens, it's okay to pause and gather her thoughts before speaking up. The assertiveness needs to happen and is not personal; it's a professional tactic to keep the project moving in the right direction.

How Sue feels coming out of these meetings has improved meeting by meeting. The first time she used this technique for a meeting it felt, in her words, 'weird'. But many months of meetings later, she notices that she feels a lot more respected and appreciated, with the team often asking for her input rather than talking over her.

This is neuroplasticity in action. A new pathway has been formed. The payoff for Sue is that her anxiety and discomfort have dissipated, and ridding herself of the constant distraction of self-doubting thoughts has injected more time into her days.

BELIEVE NOW

You now have the tools to pay more attention to the way you think, feel and behave. More specifically, to look for patterns in the way you think about and perceive what happens to and around you.

- What have you noticed about your first thoughts each new day?
- Are they positive, negative or something in between?

If you haven't explored yet, be sure to notice when you wake up tomorrow. This could be the very clue you have been searching for that shines a light on what pathways or roads are lighting up in your brain each day.

Then you get to make a choice.

- Do I need to make a change?
- What do I need to put repeated attention on to make that change?

If you are still struggling with internal self-awareness, take a breath and remember how powerful that space called the 'pause' is.

EXTERNAL SELF-AWARENESS

At the very end of a one-on-one catch-up with one of her team members, Mikayla asked, 'Do you have any questions for me or feedback on what I can do better as a leader?' The team member looked a little awkward and Mikayla wondered what was to come. She didn't speak, but rather let the awkward pause linger. Eventually, her team member spoke. 'Well,' said Mike, 'I kind of feel as though you don't really care about how I'm doing.' His face started to go red and Mikayla encouraged him to carry on. 'Well,' Mike said awkwardly, 'you never really stop and talk to me and when I ask you a question, your answers are always short and to the point.'

Mikayla felt annoyed. She was new to her leadership role and was leading three team members who, before her promotion, had been her colleagues. She didn't want them to feel that, just because she was now their manager, she needed to know their every move. She thought they'd appreciate being left to their own devices and trusted to get on with their jobs. Each week began with a Monday morning meeting where team members gave an update about their projects, and as a team they had a general discussion about the week ahead. As far as Mikayla could see, this structure was working well.

Her response to Mike didn't say any of that, though. She almost screeched at him when she said, 'That's simply not true; of course I care about the work you're doing.' What she didn't realise was that, in that moment, she'd shut him down. She still felt annoyed and 'How dare he?' was the thought she couldn't budge from her mind. She was trying so hard to let him work autonomously. She did manage to say, 'But thank you for your feedback, I'll have a think about it,' even though she had no real intention to do any thinking. Funny thing is, for most of the afternoon, that was **all** she thought about.

In her weekly session with her leadership coach, Mikayla mentioned the conversation with Mike and how unfair and ungrateful she thought he was. After all, she was deliberately giving short answers so that he felt in control and could get on with his day. Her coach, not so subtly, asked, 'Have you asked your other team members the same question?' 'Hell no,' was her quick response. Mikayla's coach suggested that she do just that and be open to the possibility that it was not just Mike who was feeling this way.

Blind spots are the gap between how leaders believe they behave and how their employees say they behave, and they won't always say it directly to you. Unless you ask.

Every human has a physical blind spot, a point in our field of vision for each eye that we simply cannot see. A recent global study conducted by DaleCarnegie.com shows that leaders also have blind spots. These blind spots are the gap between how leaders believe they behave and how their team says they actually behave.

LET FEEDBACK BE YOUR FRIEND

If you drive, you have probably had the experience of being about to change lanes only to discover that there is another vehicle just behind you in that lane which you didn't see when you first looked in your mirrors. The reason you didn't see it was because the car was in your blind spot.

As individuals, we also have 'blind spots' in our behaviour. Basically, blind spots are faults or unhealthy patterns of behaviour that continually cause us grief, but that we are not consciously aware of. As leaders, sometimes we don't see the ways we behave towards others and that can have unintended consequences.

Truth is, we are unlikely to wake up one day and suddenly see a blind spot. We are much more likely to have a blind spot pointed out to us by someone else – ouch!

When my manager talked to me about bravado, she was pointing out a blind spot to me, saying my confidence was coming across more as arrogance. I had no idea I was portraying that. No idea whatsoever. When it was brought to my attention, almost immediately I started seeing how it could be perceived that way. It was hard to hear but led to positive change.

When you are driving a vehicle, driver visibility is the maximum distance at which you can see and identify prominent objects around the vehicle. Change vehicle to 'leader' and your blind spots create a situation where your visibility is reduced and your judgement of people, places and things is determined by that reduced visibility, particularly visibility of your own behaviour. You are not seeing the whole situation.

Blind spots can inhibit your growth as a leader, frustrate your development and become a stumbling block to success in your relationships with your team. It makes sense then that the next step you take is to find out what your blind spots might be.

It's important to be mindful that blind spots don't make us *wrong*. We are all conditioned throughout our lives with different behavioural, cultural and moral standards. These standards are born out of our experiences, whom we grow up with, what is shown and taught to us. This conditioning impacts how we view ourselves, how we view others, and influences our workplace behaviour. Some of this conditioning could block us from seeing the truth about our own behaviour, stopping us from realising how we are coming across to or impacting others.

Undetected blind spots can lead to embarrassing workplace moments and unintended insults. Just like Mikayla didn't mean to appear short and uncaring about how Mike was doing day to day. As with thoughts, the same goes with blind spots – we need to become more aware of our own, and the best way to do that is to seek feedback.

Before I talk about how to seek feedback, I ask you to be mindful of your own mental wellbeing and psychological safety. Not all feedback is equal. Don't react to someone immediately when they give you feedback. Simply say thank you and let them know that you will reflect on it in your own time. When you can find the time, a private space and the energy to reflect on the feedback, then it is time to review it and reflect. Expect some great feedback, but also be willing to dig deeper for more.

INTO ACTION

It is very hard to 'fix' a blind spot when you don't know what it is, and identifying your own blind spots is a weird contradiction, because if you're aware of a problem, it doesn't count. Evidence that you may have blind spots is in those repetitive experiences that are baffling you. Those things that make you shout, 'Why does this always happen to me?' What I am suggesting you do next will take some courage. It is worth every ounce of energy it takes to find that courage, because a micro shift in behaviour created by becoming aware of a blind spot could be that one thing that suddenly generates a breakthrough.

For the next week, I encourage you to make a conscious choice to ask **one person every day** if there is anything about you that you don't see, but others do.

For those of you filled with self-doubt and who freeze with dread at asking for feedback this way, remember that some of the feedback is likely to be positive. Start with your family and friends, but also ask work colleagues, managers and your team. Sometimes those who don't know you very well understand you even more than your closest friends and family.

Follow these guidelines when asking for external feedback.

MAKE IT SAFE FOR THEM
Sharing feedback may feel risky for those you ask, especially your team. Be sure to reassure them that their honesty won't be met with negative repercussions. You can do this before you ask for feedback by being curious and showing a little vulnerability.

ASK FOR SPECIFIC FEEDBACK
While I have suggested that you ask if there is anything about you that you don't see but others do, if the person you are asking struggles, it may help to be more specific. You could ask, 'What did you hear when I shared my strategy?' or 'How often do I interrupt people in meetings?' Perhaps you could ask about your written communication by saying, 'How did it feel to you when I sent that email?'

GIVE YOUR FULL ATTENTION AND LISTEN CAREFULLY
Eliminate distractions, including your phone and laptop, and focus fully on the person giving the feedback. Having your phone present, even if you're not looking at it, reduces your ability to connect with others more than you think. Be open to listening. You might hear that you are too critical, impatient, or conflict or risk averse. Maybe someone else thinks you are too easily

offended. Resist the impulse to evaluate the accuracy of the message. This moment is about listening.

DON'T DEBATE OR DEFEND

If you find yourself disagreeing with some feedback, practise self-awareness and notice this reaction, but do not offer contradictory evidence or challenge the person offering feedback. If you debate, you will look defensive, won't appear open to feedback, and you may decrease the likelihood of that person offering you feedback in the future.

OWN YOUR REACTIONS

You may feel happy, angry, confused or frustrated by what you hear. Recognise that your reactions are about you, and not the other person. You asked for feedback and someone was generous enough to share it with you. It's your responsibility to own and explore your reactions. Instead of finding fault in the messenger, become curious about yourself.

DEMONSTRATE GRATITUDE

Regardless of the answer, thank the person for their honest feedback then write the feedback down and forget about it until you are safely alone and can assess it honestly. If you truly believe the feedback says more about the other person's outlook than your own, discount it, but if you keep getting the same feedback again and again, then these people probably have a point.

With all of that in mind, you are well equipped to ask your external feedback questions, then reflect mindfully on what you've heard.

EXTERNAL FEEDBACK QUESTIONS AND REFLECTION

Use the following question and reflection structure each day for seven days. You can do it either in a notebook or in the companion workbook.

- Is there anything about me that I don't see but others do?
- What do I do well as a leader?
- What could I do better as a leader?

When you can, find a quiet and private space and take time to reflect on the feedback you received.

- What was said about me?
- What did I think about what was said about me?
- Was I surprised with the feedback?
- Is it true?
- Have I heard this before?

IT'S NOW TIME TO EVALUATE

By thinking through what the feedback means to you, you can learn from it and consider what parts to accept and work on, what parts to disregard and what parts require deeper understanding. If their feedback does hit a nerve and you think there could be truth to it, start to look out for what they are talking about.

When I started looking for bravado, I began seeing how it could be seen that way. But I didn't fully buy into it and criticise myself, because it wasn't my intention to come across this way. I chose to pause before I spoke, lower my voice a little and be mindful of observing the other person's reaction.

BALANCE IS KEY WHEN YOU ARE SEARCHING TO BELIEVE
Some people will find it easier than others to give you feedback, no matter how safe you make it for them. But, when you do this well, you will receive some feedback that will surprise you. Given that you are here looking for tools to **believe** in yourself and your leadership, it is important that you keep balanced.

Don't be that person who hears ten great pieces of feedback and one negative one, then ruminates for twenty-four hours on the one negative piece. Equally, don't only focus on the good stuff because it feels better. Find the courage to look at all of your blind spots.

Once you have completed your reflection process, it's decision time.

- What action will I take or what change will I make?

By asking yourself this question and **deciding** on an action step, you are taking ownership of your desire to be self-aware and making sure that the feedback has been 'useful'.

If you see evidence that the feedback is true, but you still feel stuck, be assured that change is possible. This may even be the one per cent change that will see you step into your full potential. And remember, neuroplasticity is your friend. You can rewire your brain to think, do or be a different way.

CHOOSING TO CHANGE

They say it takes sixty-six times to change a behaviour, so there is every chance that it won't happen overnight. Awareness is just the beginning. Once you have that, then you can consciously choose to change your behaviour and habits.

While you can choose to form new pathways in your brain, be mindful that your brain is fantastic at choosing an easy path. It can often try to conserve fuel and stay in the safety net of your comfort zone. Evidence of this is when you feel like giving up because the change is getting too hard. To mitigate this, set yourself a goal and action steps to keep yourself on track. Anything that is worth doing is worth doing well. Change takes effort.

Dale Carnegie's white paper titled 'Recognising Leadership Blind Spots' suggests that when leaders overcome their blind spots, employees are more likely to be very satisfied with their job, more than those who have leaders who ignore their blind spots and don't acknowledge what they can't see. So keep going.

Mastering your blind spots can take your leadership to the next level. There will be a lot less shouting *'Why did this happen to me?'* and more tendency to take a moment to reflect and see the truth of what is going on. When you embrace self-improvement in this way, you are leading by example and, in a sense, giving others permission to do the same.

Simply observing the truth about yourself without judgement will begin to change you. We all need courage to see and transform our blind spots. That's the harsh reality and we might get a few bruises along the way. But when you start to shine a light on them, it is a lot easier to change your behaviour and align with who you truly are.

We may never completely eradicate our blind spots; they are part of human nature. But through candid self-reflection combined with focused effort, we can safely steer ourselves towards becoming the successful leaders we want to be.

———————————

You may even realise that some of the self-doubting stories you tell yourself are simply not true.

———————————

COMMON DENOMINATOR

Lauren is a great example of facing her shadows head on and choosing to change. She was the leader of a team of five and came to her coaching call fraught with frustration. She spent the first half hour talking about all the issues she was having with her team, who were not communicating. Her main worry, she said, was that her frustration was developing into anger and she was getting very close to having an outburst at the most inappropriate time.

Once she was onto her umpteenth story about team member number four, Lauren let out a heavy sigh and paused for quite some time. It was well into this pause that I asked her if she was willing to look at her part in this, reminding Lauren that she was in fact the common denominator in all these situations. I watched her wince, then she sighed again.

Having spent so long venting about others, she couldn't deny that, yes, the commonality in all these situations was in fact her. Thankfully, blended in with her increasing frustration was a willingness to have a look at her own behaviour and communication style. She admitted that she hadn't liked how she was starting to react aggressively with her team, partly because she was so busy, but also because she was so frustrated.

Somehow, she had got herself into a downward spiral of looking to others for blame and was ruminating about all the things they were doing wrong. Lauren almost pointed out her own blind spot in this situation, but she hadn't seen it previously because she was so stuck in it.

Once she was on the other side of her embarrassment, Lauren was hopeful. She knew she had more control to change herself than anyone else, so she glided effortlessly into talking about the solution. She could feel her frustration lessening.

She took a little time to face what she'd realised and make changes. The result was that communication improved among the team, engagement grew and, while it seemed like magic, it was simply self-awareness and purposeful action creating this change.

Unless you learn to face your own shadows, you will continue to see them in others, because the world outside you is only a reflection of the world inside you.

BELIEVE NOW

The greatest blind spot of all is the denial of blind spots. Discovering your blind spots can be a powerfully transformative exercise.

- What did you discover when you received feedback?
- Were there many surprises?
- How did it feel for you and what have you decided to change?

If you can't answer these questions because you haven't asked for feedback, I encourage you to give it a go when you can.

Make a conscious choice to ask **one person every day** for the next seven days if there is anything about you that you don't see, but others do.

Okay, yes, it might leave you with a small scrape or even a big bruise, but there is no downside to becoming more self-aware. The simple act of asking will give you greater self-insight and take you one step closer to belief.

EMOTIONAL SELF-AWARENESS

Once upon a time, a psychology professor walked around on a stage while teaching stress management principles to an auditorium filled with students. As she raised a glass of water, everyone expected they'd be asked the typical *glass half empty or glass half full* question.

Instead, with a smile on her face, the professor asked, 'How heavy is this glass of water I'm holding?' Students shouted out answers ranging six ounces to 500 grams or more.

She replied, 'From my perspective, the absolute weight of this glass doesn't matter. It all depends on how long I hold it. If I hold it for a minute or two, it's fairly light. If I hold it for an hour straight, its weight might make my arm ache a little. If I hold it for a day straight, my arm will likely cramp up and feel completely numb and paralysed, forcing me to drop the glass to the floor. In each case, the weight of the glass doesn't change, but the longer I hold it, the heavier it feels to me.'

As the class shook their heads in agreement, she continued, 'Your stresses and worries in life are very much like this glass of water – think about them for a while and nothing happens. Think about them a bit longer and you begin to ache a little. Think about them all day long, and you will feel completely numb and paralysed – incapable of doing anything else until you drop them.'

––––––––––––––––––

If you still feel the weight of yesterday's stress, it's a strong sign that it's time to put the glass down.

––––––––––––––––––

But how can you drop your stress and worries if you don't have awareness about what they are? How can you let go of emotions when you don't even know you are carrying them around?

FIGHT, FLIGHT OR FREEZE

Heightened emotional reactions are confronting. They can come seemingly out of nowhere and completely disrupt your thoughts, focus and even your days. They are also very real and happening a lot in our current changing work environments, leading quickly to issues like anxiety, tension, frustration, overwhelm and eventually burnout.

What is happening is that your amygdala, which I often refer to as the **stress centre of the brain**, has gone into overload. The amygdala is the part of the brain that is responsible for the fight, flight or freeze response.

Daniel Goleman introduced the term 'amygdala hijacking', which he first used in his 1995 book *Emotional Intelligence: Why It*

Can Matter More Than IQ to refer to an immediate and intense emotional reaction that's out of proportion to the situation. In other words, it's when someone 'loses it' or seriously overreacts to something or someone.

Goleman's term aims to recognise that we have an ancient structure in our brain, the amygdala, that is designed to respond swiftly to a threat. While the amygdala is intended to protect us from danger, it can interfere with our functioning in the modern world where threats are often more subtle in nature.

The story of carrying the water makes sense, but it's impossible to let go of something if you are not aware of it. **Emotional self-awareness** is the ability to recognise and understand your **emotions** and how they impact your behaviour, so that you don't end up carrying around that weighty glass filled with water – emotions.

It's about knowing how you feel and why you feel that way. In the workplace, we rarely share what's going on beneath the surface. At many companies, the unspoken expectation of a leader is that you park your emotional life at the door, put on your game face, and keep things light and professional. In short, you bring a part of yourself to work and try to suppress the rest.

But at what cost? The more preoccupied and distracted we are with emotions, the less focus we bring to our work. When strong feelings can't be acknowledged, they fester and get acted out, often in passive-aggressive ways. Over time, they drain your energy, individually and organisationally.

Awareness of emotions is the key that helps you understand and control them – rather than allowing them to control you. When you can master this, you'll be less thrown off balance by stress and less likely to have negative emotional responses in dynamic situations.

Studies have shown that being more aware of your emotions is linked to higher self-esteem, better relationships and less social anxiety. Who doesn't want that as a leader?

IDENTIFYING YOUR EMOTIONS

When emotions have the wrong intensity, duration or type for a particular situation, they can actually be quite harmful to us. Think about the last time you got upset about something that later turned out not to be true. Or the time you worried about something scary that might happen, then it didn't eventuate. All that wasted energy. When we become more aware of what is likely to trigger certain emotions, the sting almost magically dissipates from that trigger.

The good news is that our body will usually give us a physical reaction when we experience an emotion, especially when it's an intense emotion like fear, embarrassment, anxiety or worry. Again, think about the last time you got upset or worried about something. Chances are, you had a physical reaction in your body, equal to the intensity of the emotion. Some get tummy flutters, sore throat, tight chest or the age-old embarrassment reaction of a temperature rise and reddening face.

These are called neurophysiological components of emotions. They are the bodily symptoms that you experience during emotions. It is the process your body switches on to make you aware of the event that you are experiencing.

Other reactions could be:
- Feeling cold shivers
- Heartbeat slowing down or getting faster
- Breathing slowing down or getting faster
- Muscles tensing or relaxing

Not everybody experiences emotions the same way. A good way to increase emotional awareness is to try and determine for yourself which emotions are linked to which bodily reactions. Knowing the pattern of changes will increase the chance of quickly recognising the emotion you are experiencing. And the fastest way to become more aware of your emotions is to *pause* when you experience a bodily reaction. Take a moment to think about what is happening around you, acknowledge what you are feeling and name it. Become familiar with it.

You can use a similar reflection tool to the one you used for blind spots. If you can't do this straight away, come back and reflect at the end of the situation or day. Don't gloss over this exercise. Put some effort into it. Not only will you be less affected by unexpected emotions, but your team will also reap the benefit because of something called emotional contagion. There are no short cuts to awareness.

EMOTIONAL REFLECTION

If you struggle to pause during the emotional reaction, try this.

For the next seven days, at the end of your workday while your memory is still fresh, use this emotional reflection structure. You can do it either in a notebook or in the **companion workbook**.

- What was the physical sensation I noticed?
- What had just happened?
- What am I feeling now?
- What emotion do I think this is showing me?
- Next time I feel this way, I will…

After seven days, you will be able to identify which emotions belong to each physical sensation. This recognition will guide you closer to being able to take a pause before the emotions take over and control you. This is called practising emotional control.

EMOTIONS ARE CONTAGIOUS

One of the many benefits of recognising your emotions is being aware of what you are sharing among your team. What emotions your team might catch from you. Yes, emotions are catchy. It's called emotional contagion.

Think about this. If someone is coming towards you smiling, your natural tendency is to smile. The same thing happens when it's a frown; chances are your tendency is to frown too. You've just experienced a form of emotional contagion. By mimicking others' facial expressions, we can tap into how they are feeling and experience similar emotions ourselves.

Emotional contagion happens when someone's emotions and behaviours lead to similar emotions and behaviours in others. It can be used to our advantage and gives sense to the saying: *'Be the change you wish to see,'* or *'Lead from the front.'*

Think about the last time you were under stress and you were feeling intense pressure to meet a deadline. What type of energy were you emitting? Whatever it was, those working around and for you had every chance of catching that energy, those emotions. While I don't want to encourage you to be something you are not, you have an enormous capacity to influence your team, simply by portraying the behaviours you want to see.

Awareness of emotional contagion takes emotional awareness to a whole new level and is well worth taking a moment to absorb. When a leader frequently smiles and is kind and positive towards their team, it will inspire positive feelings throughout the office. Imagine what the work environment will be and feel like.

Ask yourself these questions:
- What impact are you having on your team day to day?
- What emotions are your team catching?

Your team will often look to you for examples of how to behave, especially during times of stress or change, so it is helpful if leaders can present a calm front. How well do you do this?

Sometimes it's easier said than done, right? It's not always easy to stay in control emotionally, especially when you are having a stressful and tough day. It's a little like meditation. We are supposed to be in the moment and peaceful, but all these thoughts keep popping into our minds. All we need to do is let them calmly pass, then get back into the present moment. Same goes for our emotions. All the more reason to practise emotional awareness.

The next time you notice a bodily reaction, take a breath and pause. Then see if you can name the emotion. Now ask yourself – 'What emotions are my team catching?'

WHY SHOULD *YOU* CHANGE?

There are myriad reasons why change must start with you. It was the American author and speaker John C. Maxwell who wrote, *'Most people want to change the world to improve their lives, but the world they need to change first is the one inside themselves.'*

All too often we are not aware that we are emotional until after-wards, when we say something like, 'Oh, I really lost my head.' Well, you didn't lose your head; you just lost your awareness of what you were feeling in the moment. It doesn't need to be like that any more. You have a choice now to start to notice your emotions more quickly.

Once you master that, you'll find that you can then understand others' feelings better and find it easier to empathise with them. What's happening is that you are no longer getting your emotions mixed up with theirs and wondering who is to blame for what. You can choose what you become emotional about and how you behave when emotions peak. You will have the power to choose to be calm, even when one of your team is not and they are projecting their panic, anger or frustrations on to you.

Of course, it is okay to show emotion, but I'm sure you don't want to get caught up in a whirlwind of emotions that overwhelm you. Without awareness, you're much more likely to say or do something you'll regret. We've all done it. And you don't want to be carrying around emotions longer than you have to. Remember the weight of the glass of water? Negative emotions can weigh you down.

You are the leader and part of your role is leading the way when it comes to emotional control and behaviour in the office. This is your chance to **choose** the change you wish to see. You will reap the benefit of having a happier, calmer, more professional team.

Remember, emotional awareness is the third layer of awareness, giving you a much greater ability to maintain that calm exterior and control.

———————————

Once you understand the impact your emotions have on others, it is your leadership and social responsibility to choose what that impact will be. Let change start with you.

———————————

STAY MINDFUL OF WHERE YOU ARE LOOKING

Dr. Wayne Dyer, popular author and speaker, takes his audience through an imagination exercise to emphasise that when we change the way we look at things, the things we look at change.

He asks them to imagine a scene. Let me take you through it now.

Imagine you are in your house and you have your car keys in your hand. There is a power failure and the lights go out. You can't see a thing. You stumble around in your living room and you drop your keys. You look around for a while, but soon you realise you are never going to find them in the dark.

You look outside and notice that the streetlights are on. So, in your mind you think, 'I'm not going to sit around here in the dark and grope around looking for my keys when there is a light on outside. I'm going to go out there under the streetlight and look for my keys.'

You are outside, groping around looking for your keys, when your neighbour comes along and asks, 'What happened?'

'Well,' you say, 'I dropped my keys.'

Your neighbour says, 'I'll help you look for them.'

Now the two of you are out there looking for your keys.

Finally, he asks, 'Where did you drop your keys?'

You reply, 'I dropped them in the house.'

'Do you mean to tell me,' asks your neighbour, 'that you dropped your keys in the house and you are looking for them out here? It doesn't make any sense.'

You might laugh when you realise how silly that is, but isn't that exactly what you're doing when you have a problem, difficulty or struggle that is located inside you, but you are looking for the solution some place outside yourself?

It would be like going to the doctor and telling him all your symptoms only for him to start writing out one prescription for each symptom. By the time he's finished, he's written out five prescriptions. Before you leave, you ask for your prescriptions and the doctor says, 'No, it's okay, I'll give this one to your mother-in-law, this one to your neighbour, this one to your daughter and this one to your father.'

I'm sure you are seeing how ridiculous this would be, but we all do it. When we are triggered emotionally, it's a natural reaction to look outside – to other people, places and things – for the cause. But it's not someone else having a reaction; it's you.

All the answers you are looking for to explain why you think, feel and behave the way you do are inside you – right now. Not somewhere out there.

I truly hope you see the irony here and maybe even have a chuckle the next time you find yourself looking outside of 'you' for the answers.

When you create a new habit of going to the mirror first and asking yourself 'Why is this bothering me?' and 'What is my part in this?' I promise you, your emotional awareness will be amplified and you'll have a lot more self-control.

Enjoy your self-exploration and be sure to return to it frequently. Be the change you wish to see.

BELIEVE NOW

Your emotions are catchy and if you are not aware of them, they will show up in all the wrong places.

- Do you carry your emotions around until they weigh you down?
- Have you ever snapped at someone inappropriately?
- Or can you recognise your emotions quickly, name them and let them go?
- Did you explore how your emotions show up as physical sensations?
- What did you notice?
- What impact are you having on your team day to day?
- What emotions are your team catching?

This is your third layer of awareness and a vital one, so if you can't answer these questions, pause and reflect when you can.

This is your chance to choose the change you wish to see and enjoy well-balanced awareness, a boost to your self-belief and a happier, more productive team.

PART 2:

TRUST YOURSELF

'A bird sitting on a tree is never afraid of the branch breaking,
because her trust is not on the branch but on her own wings.'
Charlie Wardle

At its very core, trusting yourself means you know if what you're doing or what you're thinking is good for you or bad for you. You can feel it. You look after your own needs and safety. You treat yourself with love and compassion, rather than strive for perfection. You know, deep down, that you can survive difficulties and you refuse to give up on yourself. You consistently stay true to yourself.

Part one was about developing your self-awareness, shining a spotlight on your thinking and emotions. Enabling you to be more consciously aware of your mindset and how others see you. It's now up to you to find your North Star and point yourself in the right direction. To allow what you've learned to guide your decisions and keep you on track. To do that, you must place trust in yourself.

'But isn't leadership about being there for everyone else?' I hear you ask. I'll explain that as we go, but for now, go along with this idea of self-trust and treating what is important to you with care.

Getting to know yourself has given you a solid foundation, but trusting yourself takes that to an entirely new level. There's hardly a person who's succeeded in anything without trusting them-selves first – that's exactly what the following chapters will help you do. You will learn about three levels that will lead you to trust yourself more:

1. Trusting your **inner voice**
2. Trusting your own **judgement**
3. Trusting how to change your perspective on mistakes and **learning**

It is the blend of all three that will launch you to the next step towards your full leadership potential.

TRUSTING YOUR INNER VOICE

There is this old legend of a Cherokee grandfather who tells a story to his grandson that shines a light on the ***inner voice***.

The Cherokee was describing to his grandson this great battle that occurs within each one of us. He said, 'Inside of each of us there's this battle between these two wolves. One wolf is faith and goodness and openness, and the other wolf represents fear, doubt, despair. All these things are happening within each of us, this fight between fear and love. It's a great battle, epic in its proportion and we fight this battle all through our lives. Eventually, one will win.'

After a moment's silence, his grandson asked, 'Well, Grandfather, which wolf will win?'

'The one that you feed. The wolf that you feed will win,' said his grandfather.

It's not enough to simply starve one wolf and hope the other one will win.

---

*We must find ways and things you can do
that will feed the wolf you want to win.*

Sometimes we are not even aware of which wolf we are feeding, which is why developing your self-awareness preceded this chapter. You need to stop unintentionally feeding the wolf that you hope doesn't win.

YOUR INNER CRITIC

As with the wolves, you have multiple parts that live inside your mind. Some of those parts are loving and kind, some are mean and critical. It seems the voices that get heard, especially when we are about to embark on something that matters to us like leading our team in a new project or stepping into our first leadership role, are the critical voices. They just seem to get louder.

Your inner voice started developing early in life from experiences that you internalised, which then formed the way you think about yourself. Experiences such as the way people spoke to you, reacted to you, encouraged or excluded you. Those early life experiences will have included voices of authority like your parents or caregivers and teachers. The most significant impressions are made between conception and about six years old, and a lot of the information you absorbed in that time from those voices of authority became embedded into your subconscious.

Your subconscious can run up to ninety-five per cent of the decisions you make, which is kind of scary. Your inner voice is powered by your subconscious mind – even more scary! Dr. Bruce H. Lipton Ph.D., a cell biologist by training and an expert on consciousness, says, 'Seventy per cent of the programs we download for our subconscious mind are negative and disempowering.' This starts when, as a toddler, you hear two no's for every one yes. This pattern carries on into your adult life. Think about your last performance review, where you received many positive pieces of feedback, along with one negative piece. Which piece did you think about more?

Some common negative inner thoughts include, *'You're no good at this,' 'You're too sensitive,'* or *'You'll never be successful.'* According to one study by Ethan Kross, an American experimental psychologist and neuroscientist, we talk to ourselves at a rate equivalent to speaking 4,000 words per minute. How many of those 4,000 words do you think are negative?

This negative voice is what we are referring to here as your **inner critic** and given that this voice stems from your thoughts, you no doubt uncovered evidence of your own inner critic in the chapter about internal self-awareness. As you progress on your journey of personal growth and self-discovery, you may become more and more aware of the critical voice. You then face a **choice**. Is it time to reframe the messages you are hearing inside your own mind?

Many people, including highly successful leaders, have an inner critic that becomes louder as they move into the leadership spotlight. Take the notion of impostor syndrome, where your inner critic tells you that you're simply not good enough and that, despite your achievements, you're going to be found out as a fraud. Many of us feel like we are winging it, especially if we're doing new or difficult things.

If 4,000 words per minute can be paralysing, it can also be self-sabotaging. What you experience on the inside can blot out almost everything else if you let it. A study published in 2010 shows that inner experiences consistently dwarf outer ones, and once a ruminative thought takes hold of you, it can ruin even the best meeting, or that performance review where you walked out focused on the one negative piece of feedback.

Neuroscience research confirms that most of us to do too much thinking of the ruminative kind and that this thinking is often judgemental of yourself. When you ruminate, the brain's Default Mode Network (DMA) is activated. Too much of this kind of thinking is detrimental not just to your leadership success, but also your mental health and wellbeing.

CRITICAL VS INTUITIVE VOICE

Steve Jobs left us with many inspirational quotes, and this is one of my favourites. *'Don't let the noise of others' opinions drown out your own inner voice. And, most important, have the courage to follow your heart and intuition. They somehow already know what you truly want to become. Everything else is secondary.'*

While this quote is about the opinions of others, the reality is that some of the harshest feedback and comments you get about yourself come from yourself. It's hard to be self-assured, influential and resourceful when there is a voice in your head constantly criticising your every move. That voice that tells you you're not doing it right, or you should be further along by now. If criticising yourself were effective, you would probably have everything you want by now. But you don't. Because here you are, searching for your leadership potential.

Louise Hay, author of *You Can Heal Your Life*, has a great saying that puts this into perspective – *'You have been criticising yourself for years, and it hasn't worked. Try approving of yourself and see what happens.'* Great advice!

When you become more aware of your inner voice, you can quieten down your inner critic and this will create the space you need to hear your **intuitive voice**. The word intuition comes from the Latin verb *intueri*, translated to the English word intuit, meaning to contemplate. It takes time to trust the messages and thoughts this contemplation gives you.

Chances are, you have often heard your intuitive voice, but then minimised it, ignored the gut feeling or talked yourself out of whatever it told you. Have you ever found yourself exclaiming, 'I knew I should have done that; I had a ***feeling***'? Every person has inner guidance available to them and a choice to listen and live with its support, but when you are busy listening to your inner critic, you miss that guidance. You are distracted from feeling.

Learning to quieten your inner critic is a crucial skill for your well-being and resilience as a leader, helping you better cope with the pressures of a leadership role. The good news is that you can get more skilled at noticing where your mind has gone and consciously choose more empowering thoughts. The more we practise, the less power our internal critic has over us. It can take time to form new pathways, as you already know. Your inner critic will not magically disappear. But, when it turns up the volume, you can practise turning it down again.

Remember, what you focus on is what you will see. Your mind can all too quickly begin looking for negative evidence that you are not a great leader. That you have made a mess of things. It's your job now to realise, 'Oh, it's just thoughts; it's not reality.' You will find this a very freeing move.

One highly effective technique is to use the power of the pause. Pausing to notice, then letting your critic's voice decrease in volume can be particularly useful after you experience situations that trigger negative evidence or emotions, such as conflict or feeling rejected, excluded, not heard or not valued.

I once had a sign on my wall saying that one word – **Pause**. Whenever that sign caught my eye, I was reminded to do just that.

CONNECTING WITH YOUR VALUES

Have you ever stopped to think about how every action you take is flavoured with your essence? If you can't name your own values, how are you supposed to live by them? If you don't know what is important to you, you run the risk of other people deciding for you. Low self-esteem is often responsible for someone compromising their core values. So what do you think the impact might be if you don't even know what your values are?

Values are those things that you believe matter the most in your life. They are what drive you, what make you act the way you do, choose what you do. It makes sense to get clarity about what your values are. You are then more likely to live a life that is balanced and behave in a way that feels authentic, easy and comfortable. Time for another of those deep breaths in; sigh out relief.

Everyone's values are different. Some common values are things like honesty, freedom, family, love, success, friendship, respect; even intelligence can be a value. A value can be one word or a phrase, such as replacing honesty with: 'I do what's right – not what's easy.' Or replace intelligence with: 'I strive to maintain a growth mindset.'

You choose your set of core values based on what you believe in. They are about you and for you, guidelines to live and work by. As a child, your parents and teachers will have passed values on to you. When you take time to look, you will find that you live your life based on what they've taught you is important. But as an adult it's up to you to determine, on your own, what is of most value to you.

Your values don't remain static throughout your life; they evolve with you. Some of the values from your childhood may stay the same, but you might also realise that others have become increasingly more important as you have matured and changed through the stages of your life. When you start your career, success – measured by money and status – might be a top priority. But after you have a family, work-life balance may be what you value more.

When you know and consciously live by your values, you'll find it easier to trust yourself. You'll feel better as a human and as a leader, and your thoughts will be more empowering. As a quick example, if you value commitment and loyalty and make an effort to uphold your promises to friends and family, you'll feel good about yourself and the way you are behaving. Conversely, if you value commitment and loyalty but do not uphold your commitments, you might feel a sense of guilt or shame because you are not doing what you said you would. Which voice will be louder then?

Every single day in your leadership role, you will be making countless decisions about how you behave in your workplace, in specific situations and with your team. Whether you realise it or not, many of these decisions are based on your values. Once you know what your values are, you make these decisions in a more purposeful way.

There are exhaustive lists of values to be found online by doing a basic Google search. But I'm suggesting you go deeper and make a list of those things that stand out as being more important and meaningful to you.

VALUES EXPLORATION

Answer this list of questions to shed light on what you value. You can do it either in a notebook or in the **companion workbook**.

- What do I look for in a friend or spouse?
- What do I look for in a mentor or guide?
- What words describe the qualities of my family?
- What is the one key thing I will not compromise on?
- When in life did I feel most proud of myself? Why?
- What do I feel is most important in life?
- What qualities do I admire in others?
- Who really inspires me? Why?

Now that you have answered all the questions, notice what showed up more than once. Look for repeated words or trends. It is the repetition that will give you insight into what your core values are.

Keep condensing your list down until you have about five core values. These could be singular words or simple but meaningful sentences.

WHAT NEXT?

It's not always easy to make your actions align with your values, especially if this is a new concept to you. Anything from force of habit to seeking immediate gratification can make us forget our good intentions and act in ways that don't reflect our values.

There are many actions you can take to help you change your reactions and live more consciously by following your values. Here are a few you can get started with.

1. Get into a routine of reading your list of values each morning when you wake up so that they are always top of mind.
2. Visualise the day ahead and plan how you'll live by your values throughout the day.
3. Whenever you find yourself straying from your values, assess the situation and ask yourself what you could have done differently.

It may take time to carve out a new pathway, but be assured, awareness points your internal compass in the right direction and knowing your values takes your awareness to a new level.

TRUST YOUR INSTINCTS

When you know your values and you practise living according to them daily, you will find yourself reacting more consistently – even in difficult situations. You will instinctively react in the way you really want to and walk away from interactions with your head held high, because you are acting in alignment with what matters to you the most.

This will add another layer to your self-belief and naturally lead to trusting yourself more. One day you will notice that the fight between the two wolves has calmed, and your inner voice is naturally feeding the wolf you want to win.

Oprah Winfrey, Henry Ford, Victoria Beckham and others say that the key to their success is trusting their gut and that inner knowing of the right path to follow. That learning to trust your instincts, connect with your values and use your intuitive sense of what's best for you is paramount for any lasting success.

If you can learn to trust your inner voice, it's not going to lead you astray. At one time or another, we have all disregarded a feeling and later regretted it. The business world is full of etiquette and unspoken rules. But when your intuition sends you warning signals, and you listen and act according to those signals, you will have a better outcome.

———————————

Practise the occasional pause and listen to that little voice that you have previously ignored. Trust your hunches more.

———————————

BEING TOUGH WAS NOT NATURAL

It's not always brand-new leaders who need to learn to trust their inner voice. Donovan had been part of the senior leadership team for ten years. He thought he ran a good ship. Good people and personalities, and interesting work. Yes, there were a few little hiccups, but nothing he couldn't deal with in the moment.

When he first stepped into leadership, Donovan had a heavy workload and a team of six to help him drive projects in the right direction. When his team was smaller, he helped them out a lot. In fact, by his own admission, he was guilty of doing too much for his people if they fell behind in their work. He didn't want his team's pace of work to be viewed negatively by the directors.

Ten years later and with a more diverse team of fourteen, Donovan didn't have the time to jump in and do their job for them. He relied on people on the ground to be able to 'do their stuff'. Recently, pressure had been rising, personalities clashing and, right now, two of his longest standing team members were underperforming – badly .

With an exceptionally high level of empathy, it wasn't natural for Donovan to leave his team out in the middle of the ocean to figure out how to swim. He desperately wanted to throw them a life raft. But he had a voice in his head getting louder and louder, saying that if he kept doing the same thing, they would never improve. And quite frankly, he didn't have time. He'd tried the empathetic route time and time again. It hadn't worked.

Not having time was probably Donovan's saving grace because he had to take alternative action. With 'Doing what's right' and 'Transparency' being at the top of his values list, he made a new plan. He made a choice to listen to the voice in his head, hoping it would pay off.

It was soon after making this decision that Donovan had a call from one of his team with an issue out on a construction site. His first thought was to grab the keys, drive out there and sort the issue out. But he stopped himself. Truth be told, he did not have time. So instead, he asked a few key questions and left the guy to figure it out for himself. He didn't exactly swim with ease, but he didn't sink either and learned a lot.

Fast-forward two months and things weren't perfect, but there had definitely been improvement.

It took a few meetings to get his team swimming in the right direction, but they slowly began to take more responsibility and there were fewer and fewer calls to Donovan to jump in and rescue them.

Being this tough was not natural, but the voice in Donovan's head was so loud he knew what he had to do. Thankfully, it did pay off. Team morale improved greatly and the two who were under-performing are now well on track to meet their goals this quarter.

BELIEVE NOW

Is it time to reframe the messages you are hearing inside your own mind?

We have all had the experience of ignoring our intuition at some time and you don't want yours to be drowned out by an outdated critical voice.

The pause can work profoundly here – again! As can getting super clear about what it is you place the most value on in your life.

- What did you uncover during the values exploration?
- Are family and community your number one priority, or is it all about adventure and travel for you?
- What is the one key thing you will not compromise on?

Knowing your values will point your internal compass in the right direction, and you will find yourself instinctively reacting in a way that leaves you feeling good about yourself.

If you haven't already, go exploring. Trusting your inner voice, your intuition, your gut will not lead you astray. It will lead you to believe!

TRUST YOUR OWN JUDGEMENT

Lee Iacocca joined Ford Motor Company in the year 1946, as an engineering intern. Within a few months, he asked his management team to shift him to the sales and marketing department. He loved the sales work and began to grow in his career.

By 1960, he became Vice-President and General Manager of the Ford Division. His first full-fledged new car development project after becoming VP was the Mustang, and it went on to become a massive hit among the younger generation of the time. By 1978, he became President of Ford Division. He proceeded to design and launch more successful cars. He successfully transformed Ford's failing Mercury brand.

After leaving Ford, Lee took on the role of CEO for Chrysler Corporation, who were on the verge of bankruptcy. Many thought that Lee had chosen to fail. Almost everyone was of the view that Chrysler's days were numbered. But Lee worked hard and successfully turned around the company, to everyone's surprise.

His career saw him continually make crucial judgement calls that required him to dig deep and trust his own judgement. Realising the company needed money, Lee made a plea to Congress in 1979 that resulted in federally guaranteed loans of $1.5 billion for Chrysler. He restructured management, streamlined the workforce and negotiated concessions from suppliers, creditors and unions. He introduced new products – the K-Car and Minivan.

In the 1980s, to increase the car sales, Lee proposed the idea of a thirty-day money-back guarantee if any customer was not satisfied with their newly bought Chrysler car. Everyone in the company was shocked and called the idea outrageous. They were worried that people would return the cars en masse and state any random reason for not liking them. Management was afraid of potential financial losses. But Lee had done his homework and, to everyone's surprise, the total number of returns was less than 0.2 per cent of total Chrysler cars sold in that year.

There are many leadership lessons to be learned from successful CEOs like Lee Iacocca. He always trusted his own judgement. So much so that Chrysler became profitable and paid back its loans in three short years. Lee retired from Chrysler ten years later, in 1992.

Judgement involves reasoning. In this way it is unlike intuition, which is more about the ability to obtain knowledge without using reason.

JUDGEMENT VS INTUITION

Judgement is the more pragmatic part of decision making. But trusting your own judgement can be a tough one, because it's almost a conundrum. You need self-belief to trust your judgement calls in the moment, yet you need the experience of making good judgement calls to develop your self-belief. When you blend judgement and trusting your inner voice, you will take a powerful step towards trusting yourself.

The concept of judgement can be a murky one, so let's keep it simple. The essential meaning of judgement is having an opinion or making a decision that is based on careful thought. Good judgement means being able to weigh up our options accurately, then make a call.

The first step of that process is to gather as much information as you can so that you can evaluate the evidence and weigh up consequences. Many still use the age-old technique of listing pros and cons as part of their judgement process.

As a leader, you are making judgement calls all the time. Who should I hire? Which strategy should we chase? Which product should we build? How do we solve that problem?

According to Noel Tichy and Warren Bennis, the authors of *Judgment: How Winning Leaders Make Great Calls*, effective judgement is the core of exemplary leadership. It is what enables a sound choice in the absence of clear-cut, relevant data or an obvious path. They say that, to some degree, we are all capable of forming views and interpreting evidence. They also refer to judgement as a process, not a single event.

Making judgements is not new. What we are focused on here is helping you learn to **trust** your own judgement.

YOU CAN'T AVOID JUDGEMENT

Your brain is forced to make tons of judgements every day: some good, some bad and some neutral. When you're driving, you assess if it's safe to switch lanes before putting your indicator on. If someone is trying to lose weight but they are hungry and all that is in the cupboard is a bag of greasy chips, they need to make a judgement whether to eat the chips or go and pick an apple off the tree.

What this shows you is that you have been making judgement calls for years. Putting it into a leadership context may feel scarier because there are times when your judgement can influence your career or the careers of others, but there is no avoiding this crucial element of trusting yourself.

Blending judgement with other leadership qualities is essential. Consider a leader who is amped on ambition but has no judgement. There is every chance he will put his focus on the wrong things. Like always centring team discussions on the bottom line, pressuring his team to do better, but never offering training or support. All he cares about is being the highest earning team, and it shows.

Then there is the leader with charisma but no judgement who could easily lead his followers in the wrong direction, or the leader with drive and no judgement who gets up early to do the wrong things. Sheer luck and factors beyond your control may determine your eventual success, but good judgement will stack the cards in your favour.

Your team needs to know they can rely on you to make judgement calls. If they need to decide on something important in their job, but there is no obvious evidence to help them make a clear choice, it is likely they will turn to you. What they are looking for is good judgement – an interpretation of the evidence that points to the right choice.

You can't avoid the need to develop this element of learning to trust yourself. One sure-fire way of feeling self-assured when making a judgement call is believing in yourself. And that is why you are here reading these pages, right? So, let's keep going on the journey.

JUST DO IT

Remember that judgement is pragmatic, but when you allow yourself time to pause to consider pros and cons, you will also find a logical reason to base your judgement on.

Ask yourself:
- Do I have all the facts?
- Am I missing anything?

- Are there unconscious biases creeping in?
- Have I thought of everything else?

Then, go back and reconsider.

You will also need an element of faith that things will work out. Lee Iacocca took a massive leap of faith when he introduced the thirty-day guarantee concept. He didn't know for sure that it would work, but when he blended his knowledge and experience with marketing survey data, faith was the component that saw him trust his own judgement and roll out his idea company wide.

Here are **three practical steps** you can take to be sure that when crunch time comes, you are prepared to make a good judgement call, including developing your knowledge, letting go of what you can't control and practising by just doing it.

CONTINUAL LEARNING

Mark Twain quite rightly said, *'Good judgement comes from experience. Experience comes from bad judgement.'* If you make the wrong decision, learn from it. Judgement gets better with age, experience, practice and an open mind. One of the most obvious ways to develop your judgement is to **keep developing your knowledge** and know that experience will be your friend.

You are in a leadership role because you are talented in your profession, but don't stop learning and developing because you are a busy leader. Knowledge can add a layer to your belief, and most certainly your belief in yourself to make a judgement call.

I go into more depth about learning in our next chapter. All I'll say here is – make learning a priority.

BUILD UP TRUST OVER TIME

When you're thinking about why you should trust your judgement and decisions, remember that nobody who broke the mould ever had it easy. The world's greatest inventions were questioned. Our greatest thought leaders are labelled dreamers and told their visions are impossible. Impossible stands for *I'm Possible* by the way!

Trusting your own judgement can add a layer to your leadership confidence. The good news is that even if you don't trust yourself now, with some effort you can build up that trust over time. Practice makes permanent.

Sure, there will be times you'll act on a decision but wonder if you did the right thing. And even when you're certain that you were right, there can still be unpleasant consequences. Like the accounting practice leader who tells an auditor about irregular accounting in her practice. She knows that she's being honest and correct, but the upsetting result may be that friends and colleagues lose their jobs.

Of course, it isn't humanly possible to make the perfect and right judgement call every single time. But the most effective leaders make a high percentage of successful judgement calls at times when it counts the most.

LET GO OF WHAT YOU CAN'T CONTROL
If you are a little freaked out and wondering whether you can make good judgement calls, then stop. Remember the chapters you read about thoughts and check in on what your inner critic is telling you. Is it true? It's highly likely that anything your inner critic is telling you is not true, and will only distract you from trusting your judgement and assessing the options that are available to you.

Focusing on what we can't control makes us less effective and potentially leads to the outcomes we fear the most. The more time and energy we're spending on the things we can't control, the less time and energy we're spending on the ways in which we can make a difference. Focusing on what we can control takes discipline, but leaves a lot more energy for making good decisions and good judgement calls.

PRACTICE MAKES PERMANENT

Knowing is better than hoping, but the truth is that we will never really know what the best thing is to do in a situation until we try what we believe to be best.

Robert led a team of five and had only been in the role for six months. As a team, they had already been recognised for having the best culture and creating the highest level of profit in the business. They were busy, so Robert was delighted when his manager said this business growth created the need to hire another team member. Robert immediately decided he would hire someone *just like Joe*. Joe was meticulous, reliable and would stay past his usual work hours to get the job done. Robert pulled together a job description and the advertisement he wrote attracted some impressive applications. He chose to interview three potential candidates.

The purpose of the job interview was to find Joe's double. He asked carefully designed questions to check they were thorough in their work and not afraid to work past five o'clock. After three long interviews and some reference checking, Robert decided to offer David the job. David started a month later. In his first week, David was slow, but Robert put that down to him being brand new to the industry. In week two, David was still slow and Robert started to become concerned. He'd taken David through the usual induction and training, which was coming to an end. By week three, Robert knew something was awry. He realised he hadn't made a great judgement call at all. David was nothing like Joe.

Robert had been so focused on finding Joe's double that he had missed a key ingredient. David was meticulous and reliable. His previous boss said he often worked late, so he wasn't a clock watcher. Problem was, he worked late because he was incredibly inefficient and struggled with learning new skills.

The next judgement call Robert made was crucial. Rather than let his inner critic take over and tell him he'd failed at his first big leadership decision, Robert got straight to work and offered structured work-based training to David. With a lot of effort and commitment, together they were able to turn the situation around. Another judgement call – Robert believed in David's potential and chose to focus on the solution, not the problem.

You may not make the right judgement call every single time, and this particular judgement saw Robert dig into his marketing budget to find resources for David's extra training. He learned from it, though, and with Robert's team doubling in size in the next year, he had plenty of time to learn and make better judgement calls for future hires.

———————————

Trusting your own judgement can feel complicated but when you are willing to trust your judgement and make a few mistakes along the way, you can then trust your ability to take what you learn and apply it to future decisions.

———————————

After a three-week Christmas holiday, George returned to work refreshed and feeling like he did two years ago, before Covid and all its heaviness hit. His team was excited, invigorated even. They were openly enthused about being back in the office and making progress on projects. There were fifteen in his team and the buzz in the office was uplifting.

In his leadership role, George reported to one of the company directors. Part of last year's craziness, among the Covid hype, was poor behaviour from this particular director. Over his Christmas break, George had even been pondering whether he wanted to stay in the company. He wasn't the first. Several people had left last year because of this director's behaviour, and one third of George's current team refused to work with him.

George's talent last year had been maintaining morale, and he didn't want to lose the increased energy his team had. He was acutely aware that others had talked to this director over the years and their concerns had fallen on deaf ears. Worse, this director would get defensive and criticise anyone who dared speak out. George had experienced this himself. It was demotivating and draining. Even a little scary.

George knew something had to change. The team's increase in energy was great, but he felt as though he had something dangerous hanging over his head. While he intuitively knew he had to find a way to get through to this director, he also knew instinct alone was not a good basis for his decision in this instance.

George decided to take time out in a meeting room. He closed the door, took a deep breath and worked through pros, cons and possible outcomes. He decided to be as pragmatic as he would when trying to solve a project problem. He then asked himself, 'What is the worst that can happen?' 'Does this bring me closer to or take me further away from my values?' and 'How will I feel about the potential outcomes in another year?'

For the next two weeks, George stopped to reflect at the end of each week on the directors' behaviour and his team's responses and energy, and to re-read what he had written down. There was no question. His reflection and reasoning all led to the same solution. He had to be open with his director about his behaviour and communication with the team and the issues that were showing up. He set up a meeting and did just that.

The outcome was a favourable one. Not only because George trusted his judgement and made a careful decision, but also because he had taken the time to pause and weigh the situation up thoughtfully. He didn't go into a meeting with the director with all guns blazing. He went into that meeting prepared, calm and thinking about the best outcome for his team and the company.

The director didn't suddenly become a motivating leader over-night but, incrementally, George saw and acknowledged changes that meant they were heading in the right direction. Most of all, people stopped resigning because of this director.

BELIEVE NOW

What a conundrum. You need self-belief to trust your judgement, yet it is the experience of making judgement calls that will strengthen your self-belief.

As leader, this is not something you can avoid. You'll be making judgement calls frequently.

Do you allow yourself time to consider pros and cons?

Do you take time to check you have all the facts?

Do you keep an eagle eye out for unconscious biases that might creep in?

Think back to the last decision you made that you would consider to be a judgement call. Be kind to yourself and reflect on whether you did your best. Would you do anything differently next time?

Practice will be your friend here, as will a little faith in yourself. Trust is an ongoing internal practice for all of us. Keep going.

TRUST YOUR LEARNING

One day a farmer's donkey fell into an abandoned well. The animal cried piteously for hours as the farmer tried to figure out what to do. He thought long and hard and, finally, decided it just wasn't worth it to try to retrieve the donkey. The animal was old and the well needed to be covered up anyway.

The farmer invited all his neighbours to come over and help him cover up the well. They each grabbed a shovel and began to shovel dirt into the well. The donkey wondered what was going on, and when he realised what was happening he cried and wailed horribly. As the shovelfuls continued to fall down, the farmer noticed that the donkey had become completely quiet. He peered down into the well, assuming the donkey was buried, but was astounded by what he saw.

With every shovelful of dirt that hit his back, the donkey was doing something amazing. He would shake it off and take a step up on the new layer of dirt. As the farmer's neighbours continued to shovel dirt on top of the animal, he would shake it off and take a step up. The pile of dirt underneath his hooves rose higher and higher.

Pretty soon, the donkey stepped up over the edge of the well and trotted off, to the shock and astonishment of all the neighbours.

Life is going to shovel dirt on you – all kinds of dirt – and sometimes as a leader, you will feel buried under it. The trick to getting out of the well is to not let mistakes bury you, but see each of your learnings as a stepping stone to help you get out from underneath the dirt. You can get out of the deepest wells by being open to ideas and never giving up. Trust your ability to learn. Shake things off and take another step up. You are learning with each new experience.

We must trust that we are learning from each new experience and keep taking the next step up.

OPPORTUNITY TO IMPROVE

When you think of learning, it might be easy to fall into the trap of only considering formal education, but learning is an ongoing process taking place throughout life. Equally, your leadership career will involve continual learning.

While we've all experienced learning that comes through being thrown in the deep end, sometimes our learning will be disguised as a mistake. Remember, we don't know that we don't know what we don't know, and your attitude towards mistakes is key. At first the donkey cried when he realised the intention was to bury him. What an awful mistake he'd made falling in the well.

The situation looked hopeless. But once he'd learned to shake one shovel of dirt off at a time, he realised he could climb out. Do you think he fell into a well again or do you think he learned a valuable lesson?

Making a mistake is not failing. A failure is the result of a wrong action, whereas a mistake usually **is** the wrong action. So, when you make a mistake, you can learn from it and fix it. Use it as a lesson to learn a new skill or way of doing things.

Alongside adopting strategies that will help you learn formally and from mistakes, you need to understand something about yourself that will result in a fundamental change in the way you learn. Mindset! This is about the view you have of yourself as a learner and it affects all the decisions you make about your learning – the effort you put into it, the risks you take, how you deal with failures and criticism, and how much of a challenge you are willing to accept.

Think back to the last mistake that you made at work. Even if it was a minor one, like spilling coffee on a document seconds before you were due to present it, you'll likely have felt a rush of panic and then had the inconvenience of putting things right.

No one is immune to making mistakes – we are human, after all. But if we simply gloss over them and carry on as before, we're in danger of repeating the same errors. When we don't learn from our mistakes, we inflict unnecessary stress on ourselves and on others, and we risk losing the confidence to trust ourselves.

Your mental attitude, or mindset, will play a significant role in how you view your mistakes and, importantly, how you react to them. With a **growth mindset**, you will see your mistakes as an opportunity to improve, and not as something that you are doomed to repeat.

Mindset was first described by Dr. Carol Dweck, a psychologist at Stanford University. Dweck (2006, 2009) explains that your view of yourself as a learner was likely formed way back in primary school (or even earlier) and has been affecting your learning ever since.

No matter where you are on the self-belief scale right now, we are asking you to trust your own ability to learn. Even before you see the results show up. Seeing things as a failure or coming down hard on yourself when you don't grasp a new idea or talent quickly is a sure-fire way to undo anything you've learned so far about knowing and trusting yourself.

Leaders with self-belief are perfectly comfortable not knowing all the answers, and they are naturally motivated to learn, be it through formal education, being thrown in the deep end or making a mistake.

I KNOW!

We've all heard the saying *'The only thing that is constant is change.'* If you are guilty of getting defensive and saying '*I know*' when someone tries to show you a new way of doing something, be aware that this is one of the most disadvantageous statements you can use. The reality is – the things you know today will not always be enough. Same goes for tomorrow and the next day and the next day.

You don't always know what the next change will look like. All you know is, it's ongoing. Facts change, new challenges arise. You can never think, '*I know this,*' and call it done. To do so would assume that the knowledge required for solving a problem is permanently the same. To say '*I know*' is to assume that your ideas are non-revisable, and that the question or problems haven't shifted.

Bradly R. Staats, who wrote the book *Never Stop Learning: Stay Relevant, Reinvent Yourself and Thrive,* has a memorable quote at the beginning of his book: '*The learn-it-all will always do better than the know-it-all.*'

Truth is, we're all learning things all the time, whether it's a new piece of software, a more efficient process or a better way to support your team. Continual learning helps you remain relevant and can also spark new ideas. You will be more agile when it comes to adapting to unexpected changes.

Regardless of the industry you are working in, it is quite safe to say that the methods you are working with will keep evolving over time. To embrace continual learning, you need to not only have an open mind, but also be comfortable with needing to learn. It doesn't matter what skill set you have; your future depends on the fact that you keep learning constantly.

You know there are trends taking place right now that have sped up the rate of change. Just look at our world before and after Covid and the massive topics of AI and the future of work.

Today, more than ever, you need to be dynamic, embrace learning, trust in your own learning and be willing to change with what is going on around you.

SELF-COMPASSION AND ENCOURAGEMENT

Do what you need to do to transform your inner critic into a compassionate friend. It will make learning a much more enjoyable part of your leadership journey, and help you to keep going rather than get stuck in the not knowing.

If you notice yourself thinking, 'I'm afraid I'll get it wrong again,' try responding with, 'Hey, this is hard, what do I need to get through it?'

If you still find yourself struggling to grasp the idea of trusting in your learning, here are a few simple steps you can take.

TAKE ONE SMALL STEP

Dip your toes outside your comfort zone until you feel ready to take larger steps into the learning zone. Remember, your brain is like a muscle that gets stronger with use and learning prompts new pathways. Each time you take one small step, it will feel easier than the last.

REFRAME MISTAKES

These are opportunities to learn and develop. Review what went wrong. Ask yourself, 'What was I trying to do, what went wrong, when did it go wrong, why did it go wrong?' Then identify the skills, knowledge and resources you need to mitigate the likelihood of repeating the mistake. Oh, and put away the stick. Beating yourself with criticism will not make you learn any faster.

CREATE SPECIFIC LEARNING GOALS

Ask yourself, 'How can I make myself more valuable at the end of this year than I was at the beginning?' Take a little time to assess your knowledge and expertise and look for competency gaps. Then create learning goals and take action to pursue the most important learning goals relentlessly – a trait that will be a leadership advantage.

MEASURE YOUR PROGRESS

Let your learning be about progress, not perfection, and take time to reflect on what progress you have made. Remember what I said about self-compassion and encouragement!

WORK WITH MENTORS AND SEEK FEEDBACK

You can develop a relationship with a mentor by letting different stakeholders know that you are open to feedback. You could even set up formal check-ins to have your work reviewed. Feedback from supervisors, peers, direct reports, customers and clients is a critical component of learning and professional development.

TEACH SOMEONE ELSE

There is truth in the saying 'We teach what we most need to learn.' Anyone you have had as a mentor was practising the same thing. Be open to the value you can add and let it be a boost to your confidence.

CHECK YOUR LEVEL OF COMMITMENT

The level of learning required so you can retain market-relevant skills exceeds the amount of formal and informal learning hours that most organisations offer. Therefore, make more personal time and be willing to invest financially in your own growth and development.

ABOVE ALL ELSE, BE KIND TO YOURSELF

Be open to learning. It's been proved many times over that people who have greater levels of self-compassion tend to be more motivated and more successful over time.

You need to recognise that you have a choice about how you interpret challenges, setbacks and mistakes. You can choose a growth mindset. Ramp up your strategies and effort, stretch yourself and expand your abilities. It's up to you.

GOOD FOR YOUR BRAIN

Making learning a habit and incorporating it in everyday tasks is always worth the effort. Without learning, your ideas stagnate, and your capacity to be innovative takes a plunge.

Thomas Edison is reported to have tried hundreds of times before he got the light bulb to work. At one point, he was asked by a *New York Times* reporter about all his failures and whether he was going to give up. Edison responded, 'I have not failed 700 times. I've succeeded in proving 700 ways how not to build a light bulb.' Shortly after this interview, he was successful, and we have all since benefited from him trusting in his ability to learn.

As inventors such as Edison prove, knowledge and intelligence are not a fixed quantity that you had at birth and are stuck with. You become smarter every day. In fact, the knowledge you achieve in your lifetime will be incomprehensible. There are an abundance of benefits and reasons to trust in your own ability to constantly learn and develop your skills.

For one, learning does wonderful things for your brain. Recent research has found that learning keeps brain cells working at optimum levels, which can limit cognitive and memory decline as you age (Ratey, 2001). The best part is the learning can come in any form. Whenever you are acquiring new knowledge, you are keeping your brain healthier.

There is no limit to what you can learn;
nobody's brain has ever been filled.

MICROMANAGING THROUGH CHANGE

It was March 2020 when New Zealand went into its first lockdown due to Covid cases in the community. Daniel and his fellow director had twenty-four hours to mobilise their team of twenty-five so they could work remotely from home.

The trouble was that any requests to work from home had previously been declined, so as a company they had zero systems in place to make this happen. Daniel didn't trust his team to stay productive if they were out of his sight. The thought of everyone working remotely had him frazzled.

Laptops were urgently purchased, software loaded and desk phones re-routed to mobile. Each team member packed up their desk that night, not knowing when they would return. Most were excited. There were quite a few hiccups and disruptions, but after about a week, things settled down and the team had easy access to their work.

Through Daniel's insistence, they all met online as a team at 8.30am to kick off each workday. This worked well initially, with the team exchanging thoughts about lockdown and Covid and chatting more than they ever had while in the office. All under Daniel's rolling eyes, which didn't go unnoticed. He'd interrupt and ask key questions to create more 'work' focus in the meeting.

As time went on, the team became demotivated and the morning meeting chatter was replaced with matter-of-fact reports about work plans for the day. Team morale deflated like a tyre with a slow-leaking puncture. Customers started cancelling work orders, profits were down and the team was tired of prickly questions from management. Daniel watched activity decrease and forecasted revenue disappear from his spreadsheet. He'd never been so worried.

He called together his group of team leaders to talk about what he was noticing. Near the end of the meeting, one of those leaders took a deep gulp of courage and told Daniel something that knocked him sideways. 'Customers are leaving because the team feels like leaving. They are tired of being controlled and micromanaged. No one is happy here. Remote working hasn't helped. It's made them see it even more.' Daniel didn't react well. His anger and outburst were instant. The online meeting ended abruptly and he spent the rest of his day blaming everyone, in his head, for what was going on. 'How dare they?' and 'How ungrateful,' were on constant replay. He lay awake through the night thinking.

The next day, after about an hour's sleep, Daniel knew something needed to change, otherwise he'd be out of business. He didn't for a moment think it was him who needed to change, but a conversation with his fellow director changed that. The director reiterated what the team leader had said a day earlier. Daniel initially told himself that of course she would say that; she was the soft touch out of the two of them. But he couldn't deny the fact that customer sales were dropping off rapidly and something needed to change. Maybe he'd been doing this all wrong.

Daniel changed things up. First, he assigned each of his team leaders the task of facilitating the morning meeting and sat back to watch. The personal chatter quickly returned, which irked him, but under the instruction of his fellow director he did his best to control his emotions. Next, he missed one of the meetings completely, a suggestion by his leadership team. He felt anxious and almost angry, but knew he had to try something different.

It was a hard pill to swallow and tough lesson to learn when he noticed positive change. Daniel had learned something he'd never noticed before. Trying to control people wasn't working. He didn't manage to change overnight and made a few more mistakes along the way. But over time, Daniel realised a positive cycle: when he was more relaxed he made the team happier, which made customers happier, which made him feel more relaxed.

From this point on, Daniel found himself feeling a lot more open to learning.

BELIEVE NOW

What have you done in the past week to learn something new?
Have you made a mistake, or used new software or a different
process? Or have you learned something about yourself?

- How did you *feel* about what you learned?
- Did you embrace that learning with a growth mindset?

Your mental attitude plays a significant role in how you view
mistakes and learning. It's okay not to know all the answers right
now. We're all learning new things all the time. It's a part of life,
not just leadership.

I encourage you to make learning a habit. Not only will it keep
your mind active, the next thing you learn may just be that boost
to your confidence that you have been hanging out for.

PART 3:

BE YOURSELF

'Be yourself. Everyone else is already taken.'
Oscar Wilde

You've read about knowing yourself and trusting yourself; the next step is to be it. Be the leader who makes a difference, works to their potential and takes others along for the journey. But, most of all, be you! Even if you don't have all the answers yet, you've seen that you can choose to trust yourself and embrace your own leadership evolution. Remember the chicken and eagle story? Don't stay trapped in a coop when you were really born to fly.

I love this quote by Ralph Waldo Emerson: *'To be yourself in a world that is constantly trying to make you something else is the greatest accomplishment.'*

Society can sometimes want us to fit into a mould, but only one mould will fit. This is your journey, and you have every right to shine brightly with all your newfound self-awareness, trust and belief. Choice is powerful.

Learning to be your best leadership self so that you can make better choices is broken down into three parts:
1. Be the change
2. Be your priority
3. Be visible

It's time to add techniques into your toolkit to help you embrace and drive change, to help you understand the role of self-care and to show you how you can make a bigger difference by being your authentic self. Let's look at each part in more detail.

BE THE CHANGE

So many of us have heard and been moved by the quote from Gandhi: *'Be the change you wish to see.'* But we don't often hear the story behind it...

There was a crowd waiting to visit with Mahatma Gandhi, and among the people were a mother and her young son. When it was their turn, the woman asked Gandhi to speak with her son about eating sugar.

Gandhi asked her to come back in two weeks and said he would talk to the boy then. She wondered why he didn't just speak to her son when he was already there, but she complied with his request.

In two weeks, they returned, and after waiting for a couple of hours, she was able to approach Gandhi once again.

Hearing her repeated request, Gandhi immediately spoke with the boy, who agreed to begin working to eliminate sweets. After thanking Gandhi for his wise and compassionate words, the mother asked him why he wanted them to return instead of offering his advice the first time.

Gandhi replied, 'Upon your visit two weeks ago I too was eating sugar.' He explained that he could not speak of it or teach her son to not eat sugar if he himself had not taken that journey.

Interestingly, while the quote is attributed to Gandhi, Gandhi didn't speak the exact words. The actual words and meaning go much deeper:

'We but mirror the world. All the tendencies present in the outer world are to be found in the world of our body. If we could change ourselves, the tendencies in the world would also change. As a man changes his own nature, so does the attitude of the world change towards him. This is the divine mystery supreme. A wonderful thing it is and the source of our happiness. We need not wait to see what others do.'

Here, Gandhi is directing us to do the work of self-transformation, but in many cases we want to avoid facing ourselves, transforming ourselves. After all, who wants to do that? It's so much easier to lash out at the world and blame others for our own problems and failings in life, but that's not the answer.

Gandhi is showing us that if we want to change anything in the world, we need to look in the mirror and change ourselves first. We need to cleanse ourselves of insecurities.

The beginning of change is often also the end of something. Whether a thought, behaviour, belief or job changes, we find ourselves at a moment when a phase of who we are comes to an end. It feels a lot like the ending of a chapter in a book.

Change: to replace something with something else, especially something of the same kind that is newer or better.

MANAGING CHANGE

Change is simple, but not always easy. Take the alcoholic who learns that all he needs to do is resist taking the first drink. It is the first drink that sets off the craving in his brain. Simple phenomenon, yet so difficult for an addict to do.

No doubt you have uncovered things about yourself that you'd like to change. Once you make that decision to change, something shifts within you and, more often than not, different emotions come up. Even when you sincerely want the change, it can feel like it's just too much of an uphill climb. It can feel confusing, stressful or just plain scary. Some experience sadness or even a little numbness, despite feeling excitement for the new beginning that you're moving towards.

Even without a whole lot of emotions getting in the way, our brains are wired to take the easy path. Some scientists go as far as to say that choosing the path of least resistance is hardwired into our brains. Of course, this isn't unique to humans. Everything takes the path of least resistance. Water and electricity to name a few.

Remember, however, that even though change isn't easy, life is too short to stay stuck in your comfort zone. When you have a big dream in mind, you must stick your neck out if you want to build the life you've always wanted. Each change is like a turning page. It is about closing one chapter and opening another.

Understanding the emotional landscape of change is helpful, and Figure 7.1 encompasses three phases – ending what currently is, the transition zone and the new beginning.

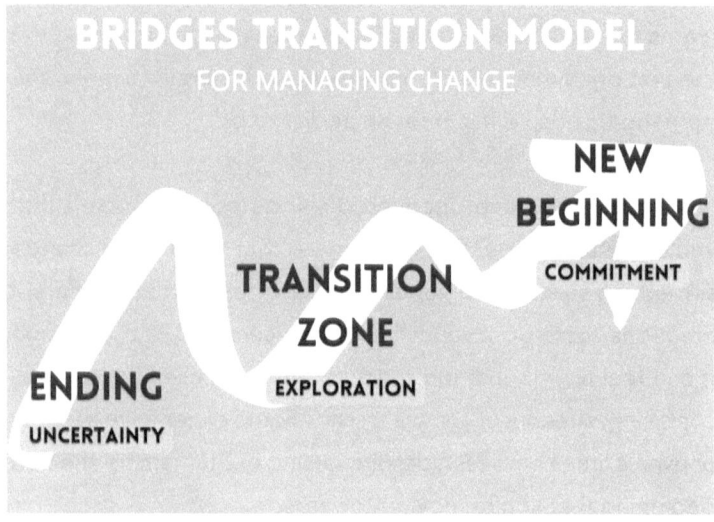

Figure 7.1: Managing change

This **Bridges Transition Model** was developed by William Bridges as a change management tool. The model acknowledges that everyone goes through the process of change at their own pace. Some are quicker to let go of the past and more excited about the new beginning.

Let's take a look at each stage.

The Ending – Paradoxical as it may sound, transition starts with an end. The first phase of transition in the Bridges Transition Model starts when you realise that the change is truly happening. This phase can be an emotional roller coaster for some people, triggering feelings from one end of the spectrum to another. Excitement and positive anticipation or, alternatively, confusion, frustration, uncertainty or even scepticism.

Transition Zone – Stage two is the central part of the change process. During this period between the old reality and the new one, what the change looks like becomes clearer and you learn to accept potential consequences from the change. It's in this stage that you can move out of confusion and into creativity. You will be more informed so will find it easier to let go of anxiety and explore innovation. In essence you are creating a new sense of identity within the change that is taking place.

New Beginning – This is the final stage and a period of new energy and acceptance. Often, this is where you will find yourself giving a big sigh of relief for coming out the other side of change. You are likely to feel a sense of accomplishment and more comfortable committing to this new change.

───────────────

Whichever zone you find yourself in right now, have a little courage and be patient with yourself.

───────────────

Although scary at first, small steps over time can lead to significant changes. And remember what I said in the previous chapter about self-compassion. Be kind to yourself through the process of any change – big or small.

SIMPLY A PROCESS

We often give up when we cannot accomplish huge and immediate change. That is when small changes become enormously valuable. One shift at a time, one step at a time, one day at a time. Taking small steps will eventually lead you to your desired change. But you need to put one foot in front of the other and get started.

As Gandhi showed us, if you want to change anything in the world, you need to look in the mirror and change yourself first. If you want to be a better listener, you can practise being more present so that you hear more. If you want more self-belief, focus more on your strengths and work steadily towards your goals.

Allow yourself to trust that change is simply a process and by embracing it, you become adaptable and more capable of handling whatever life throws at you. It allows you to continually improve throughout your leadership life and hold on to the self-belief you have been developing here.

Perhaps one of the most important reasons for embracing change is that being proactive in this way will give you some degree of control over it. You will feel more empowered. Okay, so it might not happen overnight, but consistent action will pay off.

This poem by Portia Nelson became one of my favourites when I was on my own journey of substantial change.

I walk down the street. There is a deep hole in the sidewalk.
I fall in. I am lost. I am helpless. It isn't my fault. It takes forever to find a way out.

I walk down the same street. There is a deep hole in the sidewalk. I pretend I don't see it.
I fall in again. I can't believe I am in the same place. But it isn't my fault. It still takes me a long time to get out.

I walk down the same street. There is a deep hole in the sidewalk. I see it is there. I still fall in. It's a habit. My eyes are open. I know where I am. It is my fault. I get out immediately.

I walk down the same street. There is a deep hole in the sidewalk. I walk around it. I walk down another street.

'There's a Hole in My Sidewalk' by Portia Nelson

At the start of the poem, she is unaware that she is blaming everything else for what is happening to her. She feels helpless. She starts to get some awareness of her own behaviour, but still blames everything and everyone else. Eventually, when she takes responsibility for herself and looks within, her behaviour changes and she can walk down another street. She can make the change.

Being your change means leading the way with change. Not only will it benefit you, but the flow-on effect will create a culture of adaptability. Your team will notice the change in you. They will feel it. Some will even be inspired to follow you and make their own positive change.

But how do you get started and not fall into that same deep hole over and over?

READY, SET, ACTION

As with any trip we set out on, when it comes to your leadership career and making a change, you won't get far without a map or a plan. Knowing where you want to go is one thing; achieving what you want is a whole other paradigm. To reach your potential you need to be clear and focused on what you want to achieve. You need to set meaningful goals.

Having a goal means nothing if you don't have the willingness and motivation to follow through on it. The best way you can keep focused on doing what you need to do is to create a goal-setting plan that is meaningful to you so that every ounce of your being wants to achieve what's on it. Think about why the change matters to you.

When that deep meaning is present for you, you'll make better choices – suddenly everything you do has a reason. It's motivating and will keep you on track. And when you start with a clear goal, you will instinctively get clarity on what you need to do today, tomorrow and the next day to get you to where you want to be. Wanting something and doing something are miles apart.

When it comes to believing in yourself as a leader and stepping into your full potential, you could try basing your goals on what you've read about so far in this book. These goals could look something like this:

Know myself
- Become more aware of my thoughts
- Seek external feedback
- Identify my emotional triggers

Trust myself
- Clarify my core values
- Let go of what I can't control
- Name one substantial learning goal to achieve this year

Now break it down and list the smaller action steps you need to follow. Some refer to these as mini goals.

Just as importantly, list any potential problems or obstacles that might keep you from completing your goal so there are no surprises or potential excuses along the way. Start with mindset. Do you need to reflect on your thoughts through this process? Be sure to keep your inner critic tucked away.

Think about what resources or training you need to help you achieve your goal, who you need to approach for support and how you are going to celebrate when you achieve your goal.

For those of you who are more visual, you will find a goal-setting structure PDF in the **companion workbook**.

SEE IT TO BELIEVE IT

Another powerful tool is **visualisation**. You can speed up the goal-reaching process by visualising yourself where you want to be in a year's time. Then step back to **now** in your visualisation and see what action you need to take to get to where you want to be. See yourself taking that action.

The benefits of visualisation have been broadcast for decades. Research has examined the beneficial effects of imagining future events, such as focusing on the mental imagery of yourself as a leader fuelled by self-belief. The research shows that this visualisation will enhance your motivation by helping you identify goals and develop goal-directed behaviour (Oyserman, Bybee & Terry, 2006). Further to this, social cognition research has found that mental imagery of future events increases the likelihood that those events will occur (Johnson & Sherman, 1990).

Albert Einstein said: *'Imagination is more important than knowledge. For knowledge is limited to all we now know and understand, while imagination embraces the entire world, and all there ever will be to know and understand.'*

I don't think we spend enough time imagining. Take a minute right now. Stop reading and imagine – imagine your phone rings.

- Who is it?
- Who could be on that phone that would blow your mind?
- What do they want?
- What are they calling you about?

What is the most amazing meeting request or offer you could imagine receiving? Once you have imagined that, go further – imagine how you would show up.

- What would you wear?
- How would you travel?
- How much would you be getting paid?

When you continually visualise yourself reaching a specific goal or milestone, your brain interprets that vision as reality. Visualising yourself doing the task stimulates the same regions of the brain that are activated when you are actually performing the task. In essence, visualising is like tricking your brain into acting as if that thing you want is already a reality, be it receiving a phone call, acquiring more self-belief, getting your dream job, nailing a presentation or landing a big promotion.

Because your brain thinks your desired outcome has already happened, you're more likely to take the actions necessary to align with your brain's perceived reality.

THE MIRACLE MAN

It feels like the right time to share with you a story that depicts much of what this chapter is about. It is about wanting change, facing difficult change, doing something that is simple but not easy, and achieving goals through visualising.

It was about fifteen years ago that I was first shown an inspiring story about Morris Goodman, who was called 'the Miracle Man' following his recovery from a plane crash that left him paralysed and unable to move, breathe, talk or swallow.

On 10 March, 1981, Goodman was flying a single-engine Cessna 172 around Chesapeake Bay in the USA. Thirty-five years old and one of the top life insurance agents in the world, he had purchased the Cessna the day before.

As he prepared to land, he admired the setting sun reflecting off the water. Then his engine suddenly lost power during the runway approach, and Goodman saw power lines directly in front of his windshield. The plane ripped through the high-voltage cables and flipped as it crashed in a field.

Twenty-two minutes later, Goodman arrived at a hospital emergency room. Doctors diagnosed a broken neck and crushed spinal cord, jaw and larynx. The nerves in his diaphragm were so badly damaged he couldn't breathe. A tracheotomy was performed, and he was connected to a respirator. His bowels, bladder and kidneys weren't functioning. He was unable to swallow.

His family was told to prepare for the worst. The doctors said it was unlikely he'd make it through the night. Goodman defied the odds by surviving a nine-hour operation, in which his body was stitched together with wire and plastic. But the outlook was still grim. Doctors said he wouldn't have functioning below his ears, that he might be able to see and hear but speech was unlikely, and he'd have no movement from the neck down.

Blinking became Goodman's means of communication. His sister, a special-ed teacher, created a system of cards that allowed him to talk by fluttering his eyelids. One card divided the letters of the alphabet into four boxes, each with two lines. To converse with him, Goodman's nurses, doctors and visitors would point to a section of the card and ask him whether a box contained the letter he wanted to spell. He'd blink if the answer was yes. Next, they'd pinpoint the line and, finally, the letter. Every step of Goodman's recovery was equally painstaking.

Anyone walking by Goodman's hospital room would have heard the deep-pitched voices of his favourite motivational speakers. Tapes by Zig Ziglar, professional coach and motivational speaker Bob Proctor, and positive-thinking master Norman Vincent Peale were the soundtrack to his persistence. 'When you turn on a light switch, you don't create electrical power,' Ziglar said in a recording that Goodman played frequently. 'You simply release the power that is there all the time.' Goodman reached deep within to summon that power.

Every time the respirator took a breath for him, he'd attempt to inhale, first 100, then 200, and later 300 times in a row in his struggle to breathe on his own again. Goodman told no one about this gruelling program, which took hours at a stretch, for fear the doctors would tell him his goal was unattainable. 'I refused to think of quitting even though I had no indication that this was doing any good,' he says. 'Without a 100 per cent commitment, I couldn't have sustained the belief that I could succeed.' On 25 May – two and a half months after the crash – Goodman was taken off the respirator.

Next, he focused on relearning motor skills. With neurological damage sending skewed signals to his nerves and muscles, this was an immense cognitive challenge as well as a physical one.

Goodman was a relentless patient – he had set a goal: to walk out of the hospital without mechanical assistance before Christmas. He beat that deadline by a month. He was home for Thanksgiving.

Think again about what you want to achieve and allow yourself to be inspired by stories like Goodman's to take frequent action. After reading such an inspiring story, how hard can it be – really?

BELIEVE NOW

Change is simple, but not always easy, and it is likely that we will go through a whole lot of emotions as we venture through any change.

Don't let that stop you. Life is too short to stay stuck in a comfort zone.

Where do you recognise your resistance to change?

What would you love to achieve if self-doubt didn't exist in your mind?

What step can you take – right now – to 'be the change you wish to see'?

We all have a little Miracle Man within us, tucked away safely beneath the surface. I encourage you to dig deep and connect with yours.

BE YOUR PRIORITY

Nancy was the first female sales manager at a fast-growing recruitment company. She was often the first one in the office early each morning and the last one to leave in the evening. She never took a lunch break, barely stopped for coffee and had it in her head that she had to prove her worth every single day.

She enjoyed leadership meetings and being involved in the strategic direction of the organisation. Being the only woman in the room during management discussions, and with a company-wide goal of gender diversity, Nancy was on a mission to recruit more female team members.

Before long, she had several high-performing women on her team and was encouraging them to become the company's future leaders. After they'd experienced success and shown early signs of leadership skills, Nancy would ask them if they had considered pursuing leadership positions. Most of the time, they said no.

Nancy was shocked. Why wouldn't they want to become leaders in this company? From her perspective, why wouldn't they want to face new challenges and assist others on their path to success?

After all, she found her work rewarding. But she soon learned that the way she was showing up as a leader was creating their reluctance. She took a step back and looked at what she was doing to give a negative impression.

When Nancy took a deeper look, she found that she wasn't taking great care of herself – at all. And it showed. She was working long hours and burning the candle at both ends between work and staying up late. Even sending emails at 2am when she couldn't sleep. Her days were filled with back-to-back meetings, leaving little time to support or mentor her team.

She didn't make a leadership career look enticing at all.

No matter how often someone tells you to put your own oxygen mask on before helping others, putting yourself first is tough. Especially if you have experienced anxiety and self-doubt through your life and career. Despite recognising the example she was setting for her team, Nancy still struggled with prioritising herself, regardless of being close to burnout. The need to prove herself was so deeply ingrained in her psyche.

Many people find themselves way down their own priority list like this, which is one of the key roadblocks to leadership success and general wellbeing. Making yourself a priority is not selfish! It is a must-do for your own self-preservation.

INTERNAL STRENGTH

This likely goes against the grain of what you have heard about leadership. There is a lot said in leadership articles and books about putting your people first. I'm not suggesting you put others second or last. What I am suggesting is that you set out on each new day with the internal strength you need to be the best leader you can be.

The oxygen mask metaphor is a cliché because it's true. No matter how uncomfortable it might be, you must find ways to prioritise yourself. But even if you know it's necessary to rest, make time for self-care or put boundaries in place, doing it can feel unfamiliar or downright wrong.

Prioritising yourself can be a little bit like swimming upstream. It doesn't mean you should never do anything for others, but, when you say *yes* to others, make sure you're not saying *no* to yourself. It's important to recognise that putting yourself first means that you're smart enough to know that you can't help others if you don't first help yourself.

Again, there is a huge difference between being selfish and putting yourself first. Being selfish means you are self-absorbed and that you don't care about anybody or anything but yourself.

Putting yourself first is your chance to be as kind to yourself as you are to others. Really take care of yourself so you can be more productive, have more to give and be a better leader.

LEAD THE WAY

I'm intentionally hammering home the point here because there is so much that will not flow well for you if you fail to make yourself a priority. Prioritising yourself and self-care can completely change not only your leadership experience, but so much of your life experience too. And, if you experience self-doubt and anxiety, no matter what the level, embracing a habit of prioritising **you** will ease your anguish.

Think about the great example you'll be setting for your team. As you saw with Nancy, future leaders were hard to recruit because all they were seeing was her race to the burnout finish line. If you don't allow yourself to pay attention to your own life, your team will have a difficult time relating to you because they'd never do what you're doing. Especially if you've become a person who is operating at an unattainable or undesirable level.

Add to this physical strain. You are not going to get anywhere when you are tired and exhausted from your busy schedule and wanting to please everyone around you. This type of behaviour will lead you nowhere fast. Working long hours, saying yes to every meeting and not stopping for lunch – at some point, your energy will run out.

————————————

*The way you live your leadership life
needs to be sustainable.*

————————————

Here's a thought. Focus on changing so much that your self-doubt and anxiety don't recognise you any more. You will thrive in such a state.

YOUR SELF-CARE TOOLKIT

Self-care is a broad term that includes anything we do to treat ourselves in a good way. For leaders, self-care is critical to help you show up when you need to be engaged and present. In your leadership role, you need to deal with emotionally taxing and cognitively demanding interruptions many times a day. Between the emotional labour of decisions, managing complex relationships, and switching between tasks that take extra focus and attention, you must invest time in self-care to recharge.

There is so much you can do, such as getting more balance between work and life and saying no to ridiculous demands. By adding a few key tools to your self-care toolkit, chances are you will also boost your resilience, inner strength and ability to focus.

———————————

Self-care isn't selfishness; it's self-preservation.

———————————

The first step is to make a **choice**. To see this as an important part of your leadership journey and be willing to introduce something new into your self-care schedule. Make a choice to put yourself first, then let all your energy, talents and giving to others stem from there.

There have been copious articles written about work-life balance, so we won't go there. Rather, I'll share with you three pieces of information, specifically about movement, nutrition and sleep, that can have a dramatic effect on your physical, mental and emotional wellbeing.

I have practised each of these for over twenty years, so speak from experience about their flow-on effect to more focus, energy and even significant happiness.

MOVEMENT

While a weekly exercise regimen supports many layers of well-being and I highly recommend it, I'm not a physical trainer, so I'll keep this simple. All I want to do here is introduce you to a highly effective tool you can use at any time of the day – a brisk walk.

Did you know that a simple walk around the block at lunchtime or when you are stuck in a problem can provide incredibly positive effects? There is a scientific reason why you often come up with the solution to your problem five minutes into a brisk walk.

The part of the brain that controls anxiety – the amygdala, which I spoke about earlier in the book – is one of the oldest, most primitive parts of the brain. It's also the part that controls decision making, so the two are intertwined. Therefore, making decisions when you're anxious is almost impossible and making too many decisions can make us anxious.

This *anxious* part of our brain is simple. It's a mono-tasker that can do only one thing at a time. As Sarah Wilson observes in her book *First We Make the Beast Beautiful: A New Journey Through Anxiety*, walking has been shown to shut down the anxious mechanism, so while we're walking, the anxious part of our brain can shut off a bit.

With anxiety shut down, ideas and creativity flow in. I recently had a leader on a coaching call with me who struggled while working at home during Covid lockdowns because he didn't get his commute time to wind down at the end of the day. I suggested he go for a quick walk as soon as he turned his computer off. He felt the benefits instantly.

A lot of the anxiety we see today is caused by an increased pace of life, which is not conducive to discerning thought. Our thoughts build up and up and up, and we have no time to work out how we feel. It's an information overload.

Walking gets us to exactly the right pace and rhythm to think well.

When we're walking, we're more likely to have insightful thoughts and to come up with ideas and solutions. We are likely to return to our desk rejuvenated and ready for whatever comes next in our day.

FOOD AND WATER

Everything I've learned about food and nutrition is through experience, but I'm not going to dig deep into the topic because there are too many variables, such as your body type, blood type and preferences. I'm not a qualified nutritionist and your body is uniquely yours; however, what I will suggest is that next time you notice yourself struggling with negative thoughts and not able to shake a mood, check in with your last few days of eating.

You intuitively know what makes you feel good when it comes to eating. By feel good, I mean healthy, not 'flavour' satisfied. What eating frequency and type of foods leave you feeling energised and thinking clearly? On the flip side, what leaves you feeling tired and uninspired? It's up to you to become more aware and make good choices that support your holistic wellbeing.

Water is a topic worth separating and focusing on. Why? Because dehydration can impact your mental wellbeing by making it harder for you to think clearly and focus. Nutritionist Sonal Shah of Synergy Nutrition says, '*Dehydration is seen by the body as a stressor, leading to symptoms of low energy, poor focus, confusion and irritation.*' Your brain cells require water just as your body does, and this explains why those who are dehydrated are more susceptible to mental stress. Water helps blood flow, so if there isn't enough water to help clear the toxins out of the body, you will be left feeling weak.

Do your own research if you choose to. Just know that what you eat and drink has a big impact on how you feel, think, behave and show up day to day.

SLEEP
Matt Walker's book, *Why We Sleep*, is one of the best I've read

on the topic. He shows us that people are not very good at predicting how poorly they're doing when they've under-slept.

Studies are showing that our quality of sleep is decreasing, and it is becoming a massive problem around the world. We are in a society where stimulation is everywhere: in our activities, in our hobbies and on our devices. Add to this a busy leadership role and that stimulation is amplified.

Who would have thought you'd be reading about sleep in a book about belief? Truth is, though, the quality of sleep you get each night can directly impact your brain's performance and your cognitive function. It can have a direct impact on your productivity and determine how efficient you are throughout the day.

There is so much that goes on in the brain while you sleep. Your hippocampus needs to lay down memory at night-time and if you are missing quality sleep and memories aren't filed away efficiently, then you can't recall at a rapid rate. This is when you'll find yourself forgetting where you put the car keys, not remembering people's names and losing your words halfway through a sentence. Next time you struggle to articulate something, check in with how you slept the night before.

When you are sound asleep, this is generally what will be happening:
- Physical repair takes place in your body from 10pm to 2am
- Mental and emotional repair takes place from 2am to 6am
- Memories shift from short to long-term memory throughout your sleep

If you pull an all-nighter, you will experience up to forty per cent decrease of cognitive capacity. On the flip side, a good night's sleep can increase drive and ambition by up to thirty per cent, and we all need more of that, right?

———————

Start taking care of your sleep routines and see what happens with both your physical and mental capacity.

———————

Be sure to explore self-care options that fit with your personality and lifestyle. These three are but a small sample.

You need to nurture your energy and capacity every day so you're able to act sharp and refreshed when demands come at you. By developing an intentional practice for self-care, you are certain to consistently bring your best self to the workplace. You will breathe easier, move more freely, and clarity and focus will be your eternal friends.

Evelyn knows all too well that there are more payoffs for making herself a priority than she could possibly count.

She was under immense pressure in her leadership role, with constant demands from the directors, frequent back-to-back meetings and trying to recruit new team members. All of this was going on daily while her project kept falling further and further behind. Her client was not happy and made it obvious in his tone each time they spoke.

Unfortunately for Evelyn, it had been months, possibly even more than a year, since she did anything that even remotely fell in the self-care column of her ledger. She baulked at the idea of making herself a priority. It just wasn't possible. To say she was stressed was an understatement.

One busy Wednesday, after a particularly bad night's sleep, Evelyn did something she thought she would never do. During a phone call with her unhappy client, she snapped. It was like a switch flicked inside of her and she yelled. She yelled about being 'over' the way he treated her, about how he 'didn't understand the pressures she was under', and even said she 'didn't care if he took his project elsewhere'. To make things worse, Evelyn was sitting right beside her team when this outburst took place.

Fast-forward to a meeting with the CEO and Human Resources, where Evelyn was severely reprimanded for her behaviour. The CEO had barely been able to hold on to the long-term and very profitable client, and they were even talking about a perfor- mance management plan for Evelyn. Thankfully, the company was willing to invest in coaching, and Evelyn just happened to stumble upon a coach who seemed to love reminding her that she needed to put her own oxygen mask on first.

Within her first month of coaching sessions, Evelyn had set simple goals – from prioritising daily lunch breaks and walks right through to delegating a quarter of her workload. It was in one of these sessions with her coach that Evelyn, who used to swim competitively, realised she hadn't so much as been for a walk around the block in almost a year and that the lunches she grabbed each day were missing anything that could be labelled nutritious. She set out to change this with her goal-setting plan.

What I haven't told you yet is that Evelyn visited her doctor soon after her outburst, and discovered for the first time in her life that she had high blood pressure. Her stress was the cause of her high blood pressure, which in turn led to fatigue, which created more pressure because she wasn't getting through her work quickly enough. The goals she set herself had more meaning than just keeping her job. They were about health and longevity.

At her three-month check in with Human Resources, where the decision would be made about whether or not to progress to a performance management plan, Evelyn knew the outcome would be positive. She felt like a brand-new person, had renewed energy and several of her team said she was glowing. She'd even lost weight through her renewed swimming routine.

Evelyn's decision to allow herself to be a priority and incorporate self-care into her goals turned her life around. Even when she was busy, she didn't boil up the same inside. Not only did her work improve, so did her health, and she even stopped waking at 2am feeling stressed about work.

Never underestimate the value of making yourself a priority – starting with self-care.

BELIEVE NOW

What are you willing to do to be sure you set out each new day with the mental, physical and emotional strength you need to be the best leader you can be?

- Are you willing to make yourself a priority?
- Do you put your own oxygen mask on first?
- What about bringing balance into your work and life?

Self-care is critical, especially when you are a busy leader with ongoing demands and constant pressure.

- When was the last time you put your pen down or closed your computer and took yourself off for a brisk walk?
- Are you aware of how quickly you can become dehydrated and lose focus?
- Have you done an honest check-in about your quality of sleep?

If you learnt something here, be sure to follow through with action. And, if all I've done is made you curious to know more – great! Let the learning journey begin.

Have fun building self-care into your leadership experience.

BE VISIBLE

Elaina was not new to her profession, but she was brand new to leadership. One of her key senior leadership team responsibilities was presenting to the board new initiatives she and her team had designed. Her first presentation was coming up in two weeks. She'd prepared well and practised for days, just as her mentor suggested. She'd even practised in different rooms at different times of the day, so that no matter what the boardroom looked like on presentation day, she wouldn't be thrown off focus with all the newness.

Even though she had nerves, she used breathing techniques to calm her mind. She remembered her entire talk and didn't fumble once. Elaina did wonder if it seemed a little rehearsed, but in the moment, she felt good.

It was only once all the hype was over and her mind had a chance to catch up that Elaina started doubting everything. Her material, how she dressed for the day, and even the responses she saw on the faces of those who were absorbing what she was saying. She played her talk over and over in her mind and with each rendition, her inner critic got louder and drowned out any confidence she thought she had.

When Elaina met with her mentor later that day and explained that she felt like hiding under a rock because she was so embarrassed about her performance, the idea was suggested that perhaps she was more afraid of success than she was of failure.

It was suggested she read a poem called 'Our Deepest Fear' by Marianne Williamson, in which the author beautifully encapsulates the idea of letting your own light shine and how, in doing so, you unconsciously give others permission to let their light shine.

Our deepest fear is not that we are inadequate.
Our deepest fear is that we are powerful beyond measure.
It is our light, not our darkness
That most frightens us.

We ask ourselves
Who am I to be brilliant, gorgeous, talented, fabulous?
Actually, who are you not to be?
You are a child of God.

Your playing small
Does not serve the world.
There's nothing enlightened about shrinking
So that other people won't feel insecure around you.

We are all meant to shine,
As children do.
We were born to make manifest
The glory of God that is within us.

It's not just in some of us.
It's in everyone.

And as we let our own light shine,
We unconsciously give other people permission
to do the same.

As we're liberated from our own fear,
Our presence automatically liberates others.

Marianne Williamson quite rightly suggests that your playing small does not serve the world. I believe her poem aptly sums up what it means to be 'visible'.

When you think of letting your own light shine, what emotions does that invoke in you? Fear, excitement, melancholy, determination? Whatever it is, leadership is an opportunity to inspire and influence others. It begins with you and your attitudes, then it flows to those following you, those less experienced and in need of direction and development.

John Quincy Adams said that if your actions inspire others to dream more, learn more, do more and become more, you are a leader. How can others follow you and be influenced and inspired by your leadership if they can't see it? To truly inspire, your team needs to see your actions.

Too many of us hide our leadership light rather than making it visible to the people around us. Tall poppy syndrome is real, but a waste of energy. We can be outwardly confident and hold on to humility. It's totally doable. One of the things that kept Morris Goodman, the Miracle Man, on his fast-track to recovery was a refusal to let himself be SNIOP'ed: his acronym for *susceptible to the negative influence of other people*. I doubt he'd be where he is today if he'd believed in the grim outlook given by his physicians.

While leadership starts with your attitudes and beliefs, it becomes visible through what you say and do, through your words and actions and the way you walk the talk. You will do this by stepping into your new way of being you.

It's no surprise that inspire translates to *'in spirit'*. Inspiration comes from within. Being visible, and influencing and inspiring your team, all starts within you.

———————————

By stepping into your full potential and believing in yourself, you have an opportunity to show the way, be a model of self-belief and, in essence, give others permission to do the same.

———————————

What I am suggesting here is that you take all of what you have learned and started to develop and let it be seen. Your values, your newfound trust, self-care and the leader who sets a meaningful plan to achieve. It's about taking *'be the change'* and applying consistency to it.

You'll create an environment your team want to stay in because being visible is the icing on the cake that helps you sustain an inspiring presence and create an amazing culture that discourages your team from jumping ship. In the era of a global pandemic and the great resignation, it's worth doing all you can to hold on to the talent in your team.

MAKE A DIFFERENCE

If the only reason you became a leader is for an increase in profits and salary, this book would not have appealed to you. So, I know you want more. You want to believe in yourself, step into your full potential, but still more. You want to make a difference and in order to make that difference, you need to influence and inspire. To influence and inspire, you need to be visible.

Right at the beginning I said that without belief in yourself as a leader, you will find it difficult to make tough decisions, lead meetings with authority, get people to communicate with you and be open to feedback. I'm sure you already know this, but without belief you'll also second-guess your decisions and be much more likely to become defensive when challenged. You'll lack one important component of leadership – followers.

How far away do you feel from who you were when you picked up this book? Your eyes are wide open now. You can't unknow and there is no turning back. Your team want to follow you, be inspired and be guided by you.

So, why on earth would you keep your evolving leadership self hidden? Every movement needs a leader; someone to step out into the light. Earlier in the book I shared a story about Oprah to emphasise the payoff that comes from trusting your instincts. Oprah has made a difference by letting us really see her. Being loud and noticed – being visible. You didn't read that story and think, 'Who?' We all know Oprah – right?

Don't spend time worrying about finding the right 'how to's' of leadership. Your newfound awareness and trust will inspire you to reach out for all the right tools and techniques to keep evolving. When you stay mindful, self-aware and trusting, you'll instinctively look in the right direction for what you need to improve the culture and communication in your team, to learn better delegation tactics and to increase productivity.

What is important here is that you don't retreat to the way you were just because, when you step into the office and reveal your new and improved leadership self, it feels uncomfortable. When you have the courage to shine your light, you will draw people out of the darkness and towards it.

Our eyes are naturally drawn to light. We do not keep our focus on the darkness. It's just not natural. When you choose to let your light shine, your team will naturally be drawn to you. Trust you. Want to follow you. One day you'll look back and see evidence of having made a difference.

BEING YOUR AUTHENTIC SELF

So how do you stay visible, hold on to your learnings and follow through with living your leadership potential? How do you remain self-aware, trusting and willing to influence by being noticed and being the one who is confidently leading the way?

First and foremost, you decide you want to. Once that decision is locked in, you set meaningful goals to make sure you take the right action and make it happen. Align that action with your authentic self. The you that you started to discover way back in Chapter 1.

———————————

While leadership starts with your attitudes and beliefs, it becomes visible through what you say and do, through your words and actions and the way you walk the talk.

———————————

Out of your words and actions will flow your natural ability to influence others. Influence can be more art than science, and it can be tough to get your arms around. But the bottom line is that influence matters and it's a lot easier to influence when you are being your authentic self.

This right here and right now is where all your learning comes together, because reading about belief and taking action to believe are miles apart. Have you narrowed the gap between reading and action yet? It may take a little persistence, but so long as you take consistent action, one day you will look back and realise you are being all you can be – effortlessly, with grace and ease. We don't go to the gym, work out for a week and have clearly defined muscles for the rest of our lives. Believing in yourself is the same. The key ingredient is consistent action.

I highly recommend going back and doing the work if you haven't yet. You can use the **companion workbook** or simply write notes in a notebook.

Your actions need to align with your thoughts and words for the real results to shine through.

Let's recap and talk about everything in the book that has come together for you.

Internal awareness – You were introduced to the thoughts journal. A simple five-minute morning and night process that can help you uncover insightful thought patterns. What consistent thoughts did you discover that need changing? If you haven't tried it yet, give it a go, even if only for a few days.

External awareness – If you drive a car, you know that blind spots are real. Did you find the courage to ask someone for feedback to see if you could uncover any of your own blind spots? You can always come back to this when you are feeling more confident, but I highly recommend it, as a little insight can create an enormously positive change.

Emotional awareness – There is so much power in the pause. Viktor E. Frankl tells us, *'Between stimulus and response there is a space. In that space lies your power to choose your response.'* Your response to physical reactions, emotional triggers and even your direct response in a conversation with someone. When was the last time you paused to allow yourself time to gather your thoughts or do a quick reflection?

Trust your inner voice – A simple question here. Has your inner voice been behaving or is your inner critic still playing havoc in your mind? Inner critics can be hard to shut down, but it is possible. I've done it myself and seen hundreds of clients do the same. So can you. One thing that will help you here is to become clear on your own unique set of core values. Once you quieten your inner critic, your intuitive voice – the useful one – will have space to tell you the way to self-belief.

Trust your judgement – You have been making judgement calls for years, but now you can make them from a place of inner strength and it's enormously easier to land on a good decision when you trust yourself. Practice will lead you there.

Trust your learning – You are learning things all the time; we all are. It's important to trust that you are learning from each new experience, and that inspires you to keep taking the next step. Consider creating a learning plan to keep momentum going. Learning does wonderful things for your brain.

Be the change – Change is simple but not always easy. Do you feel focused on what you want to achieve? When you wrap an action plan of small achievable steps around your goals, then take consistent daily action, you will get there. Keep going and if you haven't started yet, take one small step.

Be your priority – Ah, my friend self-care. Zig Ziglar's famous quote: *'People often say that motivation doesn't last, well neither does bathing, that's why we recommend it daily,'* is a great thought to keep top of mind here. To truly be your own priority, you need to take care of yourself. Put your own oxygen mask on first. This will create an abundance of energy for you to support others in your leadership journey.

Be visible – Your unique talents, experiences, personality, values and strengths are needed. You can shine your own light of brilliance and hold on to humility simultaneously. It may be a balancing act that is new to you, but let self-awareness guide you. Authenticity will be your friend and influencing others with ease will be the outcome.

DAILY AND MONTHLY REFLECTION TOOLS

If you check back in your **companion workbook**, you'll find daily and monthly reflection pages that you can put into your toolkit and use frequently to ensure you stay self-aware and visible.

DAILY REFLECTION

As a busy leader, most of your days end up blending into one another, so regular reflection can be an opportunity to pause and see where you are at.

The daily reflection includes your thoughts journal, gratitude list and checking in with how you are perceiving what's going on around you. You'll also do a self-care check-in.

Let me assure you, there is something magical that happens when you gently reflect each day. I could describe it for you, but the best way to find out is to experience it. I highly recommend you make this a part of your leadership day for at least thirty days. This minimal time investment will return a massive result.

MONTHLY REFLECTION

Here you allow yourself more time to go a little deeper. Scheduling half an hour in your calendar at the end of each month is all it takes. Find a quiet space, then reflect and write.

What is your inner voice up to?

What have your emotions been telling you?

How have you been living true to your values?

You'll also reflect on any feedback you've received during the month and what action you've taken.

To round off this monthly check-in, you reflect on how you've stayed **visible** during the month and how you have made a difference to others.

These simple yet profound reflection tools are designed to be a positive experience. To shine a light on your progress and remind you of the benefits of self-belief. You will see evidence of how you are 'letting your own light shine' and as a result 'giving others permission to do the same'.

Try it at least once.

There are 730 hours in a month, and I'm asking you to use half of one of those hours to do something simple that will reinforce your belief – that positive feeling you have inside that tells you that you are capable of anything.

NEVER GIVE UP

This is an extreme yet inspiring story to tell because Nelson Mandela didn't just go to prison and give up. He stayed visible. He kept taking consistent action. He went against the grain, but he knew his values and what he wanted to achieve. His goals were intensely meaningful. He was a powerful leader throughout his life.

It all started with apartheid, which means 'apartness' in the Afrikaans language. Apartheid laws separated South Africans into racial categories: Black South Africans, who made up eighty per cent of the population, were relegated to the very bottom. The South African government responded to demands for equality and freedom with repression and violence. They shot and killed unarmed demonstrators and detained and arrested many others.

While the defiance of apartheid had started peacefully, Mandela, then a young lawyer, came to believe that armed struggle was the only way forward. He and others formed an armed resistance group known as MK. Mandela spent seventeen months underground trying to gain support for the armed struggle, but was arrested in 1962. Then, in 1963, he was put on trial for a number of charges. He and seven of his colleagues were sentenced to life in prison.

In 1964 at the Rivonia Trial, he was quoted as saying, 'I have cherished the ideal of a democratic and free society in which all persons live together in harmony and with equal opportunities. It is an ideal which I hope to live for and achieve. But if needs be, it is an ideal for which I am prepared to die.'

Nelson Mandela spent twenty-seven years in prison for opposing South Africa's apartheid system. He faced harsh conditions meant to break his resolve, but refused to give up his efforts to achieve equality for all people.

He stayed authentic, visible and true to his values despite the personal cost of imprisonment.

Mandela continued to act as a leader from inside the prison and mobilised his fellow political prisoners.

After he was released, he helped negotiate an end to apartheid and became the first democratically elected president of South Africa. Since his passing in December 2013, Nelson Mandela has been fondly remembered as a South African anti-apartheid revolutionary, political leader and philanthropist who served as president of South Africa from 1994 to 1999.

And interestingly, the poem included at the start of this chapter, written by Marianne Williamson, was about African American slaves and their struggles. So go ahead, let your own light shine. Unconsciously give other people permission to do the same.

For as you are liberated from your own fear, your presence will automatically liberate others.

And never forget, it is consistent daily action that will ensure you continue to **Believe**!

BELIEVE NOW

Remember when I said you don't know that you don't know what you don't know? Well, now you do know. You know more about yourself than you did at the beginning of Chapter 1.

It's your responsibility to hold on to that knowing and keep believing in yourself.

- Are you ready to step up and into your full potential as a leader?
- Do you feel equipped to influence and inspire?
- What will it mean to you when you look back in three months' time and see what a difference you've made, all because you had the courage to be visible and show your best leadership self to the world?

It's now up to you to take consistent daily action so you always believe. Believe in yourself, believe in your potential and believe in the amazingly positive impact you can have on others by being the best leader you can be.

GRATITUDE

I've chosen to use this final chapter to share something special and very close to my heart. It's a practice I do daily and a tool I've found super helpful in terms of growing belief. It is even more helpful for holding on to the belief I've found.

I'm talking about the practice of **gratitude**.

Right now, in this moment, my gratitude is to you. Thank you. Thank you for trusting me to guide you on this journey. Thank you for allowing yourself to be a little vulnerable and digging deep to find the belief that was within you all along.

Ralph Waldo Emerson describes gratitude graciously, suggesting that you: *'Cultivate the habit of being grateful for every good thing that comes to you, and give thanks continuously. And because all things have contributed to your advancement, you should include all things in your gratitude.'*

I take it a step further by directly suggesting you find reasons to be grateful even in the things that happen or come to you that are not so good. There is good to be found in every situation.

Gratitude is a tremendous component of positively reframing thoughts. No matter how dire a situation, there is always something for which to be grateful.

I used to wonder whether happy people were grateful or grateful people were happy. This debate has been around since the time of Socrates, and while I can't offer you a scientific answer, I can say that gratitude certainly puts me in a happier place.

INFINITE BENEFITS

Studies show a connection between gratitude and physical well-being. One study in particular showed that gratitude is good for your heart (Mills et al., 2015). Gratitude lowers blood pressure, decreases stress and improves sleep. Other studies have shown that a successful practice in gratitude can lessen symptoms of depression and anxiety.

As someone who had self-doubt oozing throughout every segment of her life only a few decades ago, and as someone who has overcome major hurdles personally and professionally, including impostor syndrome, social anxiety and addiction, **gratitude** was the constant thing that pulled me through and out the other side.

My daily gratitude practice has been the tool that added another layer of positivity and belief, long after I had developed self-awareness, trust and the courage to put myself out there as a leader. It is the tool that gets me through the tougher times with grace and ease.

I see the emotion of gratitude as the special sauce everyone needs to add to their life. In fact, if you phone me and get my answer message, you'll be invited to share one thing you are grateful for today. By focusing on what you do have, you can enjoy the spark of gratitude and the reality of the blessings that are already there.

THEN THERE WAS COVID

It was in March 2020, as we entered our first Covid lockdown in New Zealand, that I reaped the huge benefit of my gratitude practice.

With many unknowns upon us all, a lot of business owners were afraid and some people even feared for their jobs. Leaders and employers rapidly needed to make sure their teams had the technology to work at home. Many of them went into a spin, ruminating whether projects and productivity would continue BAU. I had to postpone most of my group training sessions as my clients navigated what was quickly being termed the new normal. My business was only two and a half years old and my 2020 calendar had been jammed full.

Amazingly, I didn't go into fear or self-doubt. I simply continued with my daily gratitude journal. I focused on all the good stuff, no matter what the circumstances, and I did that every single day. Things to be grateful for are what I looked for, so that is what I saw.

I've gone back to my journal of the first few days of our first lockdown to share with you here. This is my list on day two. Truth is, I'd woken feeling a little sad and unsure about my business, but within minutes I felt better. As I re-read it to share with you here, I had gentle tears of gratitude prickling behind my eyes.

My Gratitude Journal – 27 March, 2020

- *I'm grateful we moved into our new home this week.*
- *I'm grateful for my family, that they are all safe right now and have warm homes filled with love and comfort.*
- *I'm grateful for my parents teaching me optimism and a positive outlook.*
- *I'm grateful I was able to video-call and wish Tyrese (my grandson) a happy third birthday and see his room filled with balloons.*
- *I'm grateful I have space in my calendar to design a free webinar series to contribute to the wellbeing of our nation.*
- *I'm grateful my new WIFI connection held out, most of the time.*
- *I'm grateful we have all we need to hunker down and stay home.*
- *I'm grateful I have many exercise options to do at home.*
- *I'm grateful for the sunshine and nature, the birdsong and the lemon tree laden with ripe lemons.*
- *I'm grateful we have extra time together in the morning just to 'be'.*
- *I'm grateful for possibility!*

My evening reflection: This turned into an amazingly busy day. I made all the calls I was to make, spoke to people who appreciated the calls and held on to my focus all day. It felt great. I feel blessed.

By maintaining a self-care practice and a grateful outlook, I was able to be present and focus on my clients' needs as many of them struggled in their leadership roles while working with remote teams. I kept on doing what I do best and even picked up new clients along the way. So much so that I needed to hire talent to work alongside me.

I know without a doubt it's my daily gratitude practice that has brought a whole new level of self-belief into my world. I know I'll be okay, better than okay, no matter what. There is so much to believe in, and chances are that one day I'll find a whole new level of potential I didn't even know I had. Life is like that – especially when you look for it.

There is always, always, always something to be grateful for.

Zig Ziglar, well known author and motivational speaker, says it well. *'The more you recognise and express gratitude for the things you have, the more things you will have to express gratitude for.'* And he is 100 per cent correct.

MY CLOSING MESSAGE TO YOU

As you near the final page of your reading journey here, there is no need for your experience to end. In fact, I urge you to continue with your self-exploration and reflection practices.

It truly is up to you now to implement changes within.

Be bold and start a gratitude practice. Perhaps first on your list is being grateful that you read this book, followed closely by being grateful it inspired you to take meaningful and positive action.

Flick back to **Chapter 9** for a recap of what we covered. Keep your bookmark there and return to it every now and then.

To give you a head start with your gratitude practice, I have a bonus tool to help you wrap gratitude around your leadership journey.

The process I use daily has been recorded and uploaded for you. You can access it within your **companion workbook** – or type this link directly into your browser: https://leadershipreboot .thinkific.com/courses/gratitude-reboot.

Have fun with it – **I believe in you! My wish for you is that you believe in you too.**

WHERE TO FROM HERE?

For those of you who'd love to continue your inner discovery and explore working directly with me as a client, you can check out the options on our website: www.leadership-reboot.co.nz or dive straight in and book a complimentary discovery call so we can chat.

Even if you just feel like reaching out to say hi or give feedback, it always brightens my day to hear from leaders who are embracing change and doing the internal work it takes to make a bigger difference.

To make direct contact, call or email me:
brenda@leadership-reboot.co.nz
NZ +6498130198

Wishing you a journey filled with exciting discovery and ongoing gratitude!

Brenda xo

REFERENCES

Page 16 – Poppenk, Jordan (2020) 'News Release - Queen's University researchers uncover brain-based marker or "thought worms" that show we have more than 6,000 thoughts each day'. Queens University Mediacentre

Page 22 & 26 – Dale Carnegie & Associates, Inc. (2017) White-paper: *Recognizing Leadership Blind Spots.* Dale Carnegie.com

Page 28 – Goleman, Daniel (1995) *Emotional Intelligence: Why It Can Matter More Than IQ.* Bloomsbury

Page 34 – Kross, Ethan (2021) *Chatter: The Voice in Our Head, Why It Matters and How to Harness It.* Crown Publishing Group

Page 47 – Dweck, Carol (2006) *Mindset.* Random House

Page 47 – Staats, Bradly R. (2018) *Never Stop Learning: Stay Relevant, Reinvent Yourself and Thrive.* Harvard Business Review Press

Page 48 – Ratey, J. (2001) *A User's Guide to the Brain.* Knopf Doubleday Publishing Group

Page 53 – Bridges, William (2004) *Transitions: Making Sense of Life's Changes.* Da Capo Lifelong Books

Page 57 – Nelson, Portia (1993) 'There's a Hole in My Sidewalk' from *There's a Hole in My Sidewalk: The Romance of Self-Discovery* by Portia Nelson. Copyright © 1993 by Portia Nelson. Reprinted with the permission of Beyond Words/Atria Books, Simon & Schuster, Inc. All rights reserved.

Page 62 – Walker, Matt (2017) *Why We Sleep.* Scribner

Page 69 – Williamson, Marianne (1996) *A Return to Love: Reflections on the Principles of 'A Course in Miracles'.* HarperOne; Reissue edition. The poem 'Our Deepest Fear' is reproduced in this book with permission from The Williamson Institute.

Page 73 – Mills, P. J., Redwine, L., Wilson, K., Pung, M. A., Chinh, K., Greenberg, B. H., … Chopra, D. (2015) *The Role Of Gratitude in Spiritual Well-Being in Asymptomatic Heart Failure Patients.* American Psychological Association

ACKNOWLEDGEMENTS

This writing journey has been bigger than I could ever have imagined. When I first set out, the overwhelm was stifling and made progress slow. Then I discovered Kelly Irving, my book coach. It was Kelly's dynamic writing structure, expert guidance and endless reassurance and encouragement that moved me from telling myself 'I'll never do this again' to 'I can't wait to write the next one.' Thank you, Kelly.

To every coach who has guided and supported me, shared tools with me and helped me overcome self-doubt hurdles and reach my own level of belief, thank you; Liza, Fiona, Mike and Landi, you are all exceptional humans and our chats gave me meaningful material for this project.

To my special friends who helped pick me up when life fell apart: Marg, Lynn, Lisa and Carol, you loved me back to wellbeing. And to my writing buddy Cathy: you've been a constant encourager during our Saturday writing stints, always excited about my updates, no matter where you are on your own writing journey.

I'd also like to thank my loyal clients who continually embrace the work captured within these pages, proving to me time and time again that my messages are useful.

Family is my number one value, so it's apt to thank my mum and dad. I'm grateful you taught me optimism and instilled in me the work ethic that it took to complete this project. I know that came from both of you. And my daughter Aleesha: my heartfelt thanks for every Nanny B Friday that made sure I took a much-needed writing rest each week, not to mention being an amazing mum and raising our future leaders, Mia and Tyrese.

Special thanks must go to Attila for just getting on with it when I couldn't be there, accepting my many writing weekends and never complaining about my disruptive, keyboard-tapping 4am starts. For listening to my passionate talks at the end of an exciting writing day or my gloomier chats when I doubted myself as an author. Your lovingly clumsy words of encouragement worked every time. When you had your accident, we learned about gratitude to a whole new level. Today, I share gratitude with everyone and am proud that it's a key message in this book that you helped shape.

Finally, gratitude and thanks to you, the reader. Thank you for trusting me to guide you on this journey. Thank you for searching and thank you for choosing to **Believe**.